London Midland Fireman

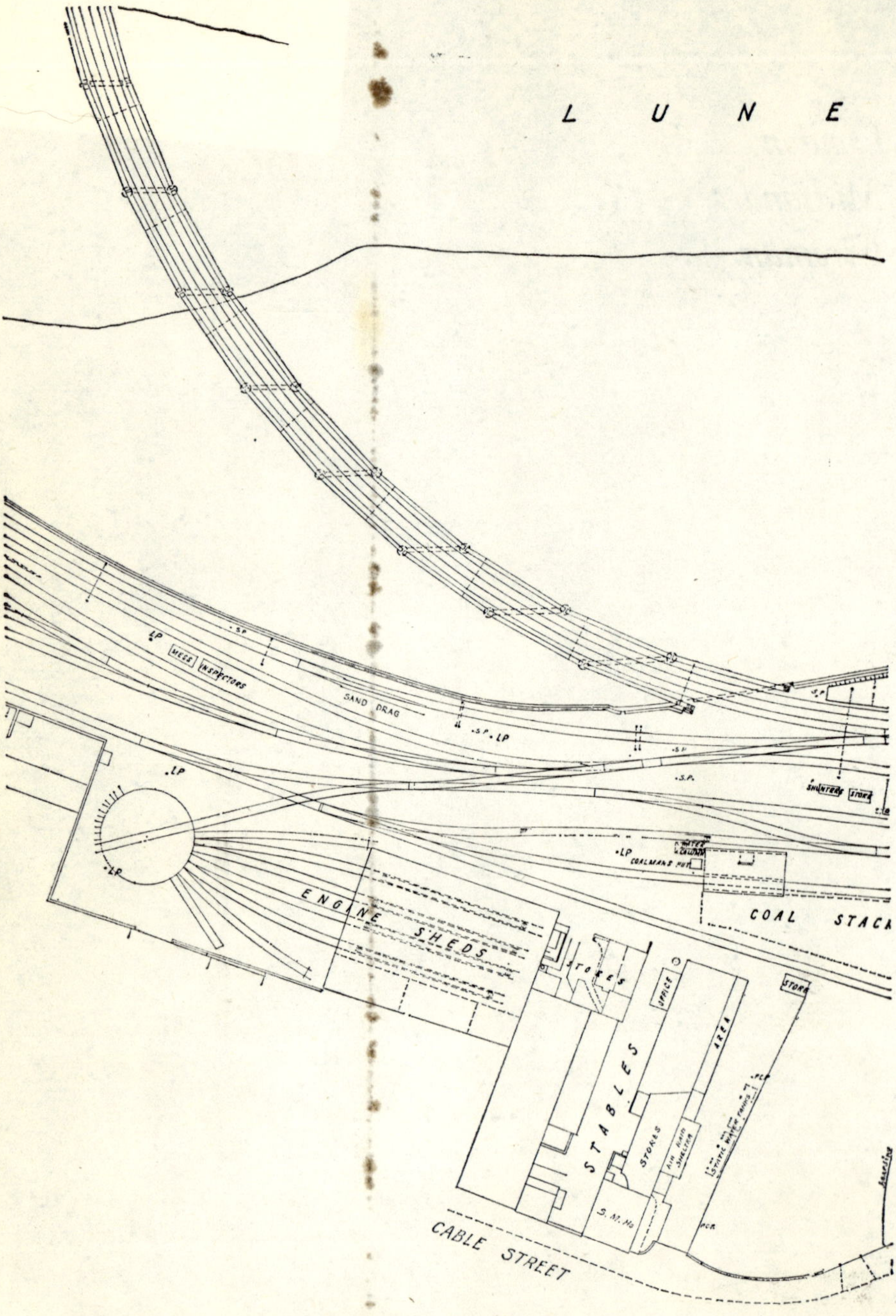

Plan showing main area of Lancaster Green Ayre Shed. (B. Rail)

M. F. HIGSON

London Midland Fireman

LONDON

IAN ALLAN

First published 1972

SBN 7110 0321 1

Published by Ian Allan Ltd, Shepperton, Surrey and printed in the United Kingdom by Cox & Wyman Ltd, London, Fakenham and Reading

Contents

This book is dedicated to
40362, 41107, 42893, 42895, 43261,
43562, 46162, 46225 *and* 58246

Foreword

Of the innumerable railway books published since railways first came into their own very few have had anything to say about life at the 'front end' of the train. Many books and articles on locomotive performance, compiled to satisfy the demands of enthusiasts, doubtless are of the utmost importance, but I feel that they have served to create an aura about certain types of locomotives rather than about the men who have manned them. So ardent have been the worshippers of the steam locomotive that the physical effort involved in its performance has been side-tracked, if indeed it has been appreciated at all. With but one learned professor crying in the wilderness, few people, if any, appear to have given the fireman his rightful due in respect of the part that he has played in the work of the steam locomotive. Indeed, I might go so far as to say that the fireman has more often figured as the scapegoat when things have not gone as satisfactorily as the enthusiast might have wished.

In this book the views expressed are mainly my own, though the experiences described will be commonplace to many enginemen. The story is hardly a tribute to such worthies as Bill Hoole or Laurie Earl, but rather to the thousands of 'Jack Jones' of the footplate who got on with the bulk of engine working despite the neglect of the many and the glory heaped on the few. It may, moreover, serve to balance the picture somewhat when read in conjunction with books on the history and performance of the steam locomotive.

Unlike many authors, I have few people to thank directly for any particular contribution to this book other than the drivers, too numerous to mention, who displayed considerable interest in me as a young fireman, and taught me, as well as they were able, how best to manage my job. I had some splendid drivers to work with, and to them I am extremely grateful. One personal tribute is to Joe Hopwood, the shed-master at Lancaster Green Ayre, who helped me more than anyone else to stick to the job at the most difficult time—the beginning!

M. F. Higson

1

A Learner at Lancaster Green Ayre

When I left school I had but one ambition—it was to work on the footplate. My longing to become an engineman was easily satisfied, for at the time there were plenty of vacancies for engine cleaners. In a comparatively short time promotion was attainable to the rank of fireman or at least passed cleaner (that is, passed to act as fireman). After a medical examination I reported for duty at my local engine-shed, Lancaster Green Ayre.

This shed was a small, inconveniently sited building just west of the station of the same name, and it could house some 12 to 14 engines. With an allocation of 35 to 40 engines it had outgrown itself somewhat, and to cope with all the engines which used it recourse had to be made to several lines adjacent to the shed—lines originally intended for use by the goods department.

The shed building itself contained four roads, with a further line leading into the repair-shop and had a short slip road alongside. The stores and sand-shed were reached from within the shed and a small separate building accommodated the foreman's office, time clerk, chief clerk and the mess-room, the latter most aptly named. It was a very ramshackle affair with a partially flagged floor, benches, a few tables and an old iron stove as a centre-piece. Surrounding this were whitewashed walls on which were fixed numerous attachments for the stowing of garments, 'snap-boxes', cans and an array of canvas lunch bags. This miserable little hovel was the centre of the shed's social life, acting as dining-hall, rest-room, card-room, betting-shop and cleaner's playground—often all at once. An ex-driver, made redundant from the footplate by failing sight, acted as mess-room orderly. He deserved a medal!

While I was technically employed as a cleaner, general labouring was more the order of the day, and the clearing of the ash-pit was my prime concern. The first few months were spent almost solely on this occupation. The engines were cleared at about 7am, and until about midday continuous shovelling was required. First, the pit had to be emptied and this usually involved liberal dousing of the red hot clinkers with the hosepipe. This caused clouds of dust and generated acid fumes which somehow bit deeply into one's lungs and will remain a memory for ever! The burning sensation on the soles of one's boots soon lost its novelty. That side of the pit on which the ashes had to be tipped was partly bricked and partly soft ashes, making the task of loading the daily tip wagons a most laborious business. Shovelling clinker and ashes from a soft ash base was much more difficult than from a hard brick surface. The size of the wagons also did not help. I calculated the capacity of these in planks rather than in tons, and it was hard work to fill from ground level an 'eight-planker' when the stage had been reached for the side flap to be lifted. On Monday mornings, especially during the summer months, the amount of ash was trebled and towards the middle of July the task usually got the better of all concerned and a veritable mountain of spoil loomed up to greet the none-too-anxious labouring staff.

As an alternative, another job of a similarly arduous nature was provided—coal-stage labouring. This entailed the filling of tubs, each of about 4cwt capacity, hoisting them with the help of a modest electric crane on to the engine tenders. It was not uncommon to handle over 20 tons of coal per man per shift. Coaling shovels were far from modest in size and would put even a Western Region firing shovel to shame. This job was very dusty and required almost constant shovelling. It was also dangerous and in the course of time trapped many hands and gashed many arms.

It was on the coal stage that I first learned a little about the types of coal to be encountered. Lancaster was blessed with the widest range of coals that it was possible to imagine. Sometimes wagons loaded with lumps the size of tombstones were handled, while at other times it was, to all intents and purposes, slack and small nuts. In between there were mixed cobbles, briquette mixtures, imported coals, cannel and what was affectionately referred to as 'Wigan blind'. This was a remarkable sticky grey substance. To illustrate what I mean, as soon as the wagon doors were released, normal coals would cause something of a minor avalanche, and incidentally make the filling of the first few tubs quite easy; but not 'Wigan'. This pudding-like mixture had to be dug out with pick and shovel and resembled the dross in a slate quarry. Right to the bottom of the wagon, this grey-coloured, putty-like substance clung limpet-like to the boards (I was to discover later that it clung to firebars in almost the same way, only more like concrete). Other problems frequently encountered were large amounts of colliery fuse-wire, bits of pit-props, the odd detonator and, worst of all, wagons with wooden floors that had become hollow-grooved and broken up with wear and tear. This made shovelling a very hard business and could double the time needed for emptying. Steel wagons were vastly preferable, and there was much competition between the coalmen to acquire them to work in.

Day after day I crawled home, filthy, begrimed and soaked in sweat. Hands which had once been soft and smooth became hard and leathery. Up till now, I had worked in my own clothing, official issue not being supplied for the first few months. My general external condition resembled that of a super-tramp—rags and tatters and, what for me became almost a trade mark, tattered trouser-bottoms.

Other little labouring chores included loading and unloading firebricks, engine springs, scrap and drums of oil. Several times I became disheartened and being unable to see myself working on engines I seemed doomed to a life of constant labouring. I had one good friend however—the shed-master, who took a great interest in me, always called me by my Christian name, and constantly encouraged me. "Mike, give a hand on the coal deck, one of the lads has failed to turn up," he would say, or "Mike, do an hour on the pit"; or "Mike, turn so-and-so engine with me". He regarded me as a good worker and so, despite the apparent misery of my position, I felt important and that was all that really mattered. Apart from these manual tasks I also did a spell of tube-blowing, arch and firebox cleaning, and a host of miscellaneous duties connected with shed and engine management. The tube-blowing was performed with a steam lance connected to a valve provided for the purpose on the side of the engine smokebox. It was an unpleasant task, for the blockage in some tubes resulted in one's being sprayed at high pressure with showers of tiny, sharp cinders which conveniently lodged themselves all over one's person. The engines more commonly dealt with were the compounds, which seemed to get booked very often for 'not steaming'.

After some six months of general labouring I had occasionally a little engine-cleaning as light relief. However, this did not appeal very much, for whatever one did to an engine it still seemed to remain a filthy object. There were numerous difficulties connected with cleaning. Engines were not cleaned in rotation but as and when cleaners were available; furthermore, cleaning materials were quite inadequate for the task. The use of cotton waste on the LMR had been stopped and instead sponge-cloths (a very inferior dishcloth) were provided—on a strictly rationed basis. The cleaning fluid was paraffin and with this one proceeded to produce a delightfully tarry mess. For the most filthy portion, i.e. wheels, motion and springs, small metal scrapers were provided. Personally, I felt that a blow-lamp might have been more suitable. As an experiment, I once tried hot soapy water but the result was even less encouraging.

The cleaning of locomotives was without doubt a thankless, heartless and filthy business. The end result was always the same—a grey smeary form which looked twice as bad a day later. The only splash of cleanliness was when the smokeboxes were blackened and the smokebox numbers whitened. The 'blacking' of smokeboxes was contrived with a pitch-like black paint applied with something resembling the end of a rope. The smokebox number whitening was a pleasant business and left room for a little personal imagination and adornment. This, however, came under notice, and the District Motive Power Superintendent ordered activities in this direction to be curtailed.

After what had seemed years of these and similar duties, about a dozen of the senior cleaners were detailed to attend classes with a view to acquiring a basic knowledge of the locomotive and pertinent sections of the Rule Book (the latter, incidentally, had been provided at about the same time as the first set of overalls, and until now had remained firmly closed). The 'school' was located at Carnforth, which was the headquarters shed of the district, and was carried on in an old coach fitted out with benches, a long table, blackboard and sundry pieces of locomotive anatomy. Our instructor was a locomotive inspector and gradually, and with seemingly endless patience, the mysteries of the locomotive were explained. The injector, brake and various forms of valve-gear were dealt with, then fundamental principles of firing and, finally, rules affecting footplate staff and the working of trains. If I remember correctly, we had some eight lessons, followed by a practical test devoted mainly to hand-signals, or how to interpret a shunter's instructions. Undoubtedly the most important matter drilled into us was the question of boiler safety and the proper testing of the gauge-glasses. Thus armed, we all awaited confidently our first firing turns. Nothing would be too difficult, we thought, though most of us secretly expected troubles ahead, no matter how confident we were, and the most important lesson was yet to come—footplate discipline.

At this point it will be as well to enumerate the various shunting and trip duties worked by Lancaster Green Ayre, and the types of engine involved. They were as follows:

Lancaster London & North Western Section

CASTLE SHUNT: This was arranged to work the goods-yard at Castle Station on the up side of the main line. The not very extensive duties here were supplemented by intermittent use of the engine concerned as a banker for heavy trains departing south up the 1 in 100 from the station to Lancaster No 1 signalbox. Other duties at Lancaster Castle which sometimes required an engine were the Old Yard, one-time terminus of the Lancaster and Preston line, which branched from the main line at Lancaster No 1, and the warehouse-shunt, necessary when heavy traffic was beyond the capacity of the Castle Yard shunter.

QUAY SHUNT: To complete the LNW Section duties there was the Quay shunt and the engine for the Glasson Dock branch. This duty involved shunting the Gas-works siding on the Quay and the sidings of a nearby linoleum factory, with an occasional trip to Glasson Dock.

Lancaster Midland Section

LADIES' WALK SHUNT: This yard provided for marshalling goods and empties for destinations east of Lancaster, acquiring traffic locally by way of transfer from the London and North Western section, and also making up trains with traffic from Morecambe and Heysham, not covered by direct service. Trains of coal empties also started from here.

NEW ZEALAND YARD SHUNT: This dealt with incoming traffic terminating at Lancaster. Like Ladies' Walk, but in reverse, traffic destined for Morecambe and Heysham and not provided with a through service was marshalled and worked by trip-engines two or three times a day, dependent on requirements. A substantial transfer of traffic to the LNW section took place, worked up to the Castle Yard by their shunt-engine or any trip-engine. These two-yard shunts were supplemented as required by an engine which worked the coal-yard, the cattle-dock and the Midland section goods warehouse adjacent to the shed.

HEYSHAM AND MOSS SIDINGS: Heysham had two shunts—the South Side and the North Side. South Side shunt worked the Quay and adjacent yards, arranging vans for unloading, removing empties and so on. North Side shunt marshalled outgoing traffic and empties. These two shunts were supplemented by a Cattle-dock shunt and the 'tip'-engine, which was provided for shunting permanent way spoil trains around the vast ballast tip near the station. The Heysham South and North shunts were quite arduous, and were manned all round the clock.

Near Heysham, the large Moss Sidings of Imperial Chemical Industries and Shell–Mex provided a large output of traffic and consequent inflow of empties. Much of the Green Ayre freight workings originated with traffic to and from Moss Sidings. The shunting turn here worked two shifts. The sheer weight of the work demanded the use of a 4F 0–6–0 for this turn, probably the most exacting of all the Lancaster shunts. Complimentary to the shunting duties were the trip workings involving transfer traffic between Lancaster Green Ayre, Castle and Heysham Moss and Harbour Yards, involving one or two engines and in part utilising the shunt-engine *en route* to the yards. To the best of my recollection Green Ayre had only one pick-up freight—the Bentham pick-up, which collected or left traffic at Caton, Claughton brick-works, Hornby and Bentham.

There were next the ballast turns. Two separate ballast trains worked from Lancaster, the Midland and the LNW. The Midland ballast worked the area between Heysham, Morecambe Promenade, Clapham Junction (the Yorkshire variety!) and the Wennington–Carnforth line. The LNW train worked principally between Lancaster Castle and Preston, and the branches to Morecambe Euston Road, Hest Bank and Glasson Dock. In conjunction with these duties was the running of the Engineer's Saloon, southwards to Preston and on to Blackpool and Fleetwood (including the remains of the Garstang & Knott End Railway), and northwards to Carlisle and occasional trips to the Cockermouth, Keswick and Penrith line and then over the Settle and Carlisle line to Settle Junction and so back via Clapham to Lancaster.

Next in order of importance were the main-line freight workings, almost all of which took place over the Midland line. The bulk of this traffic consisted of oil and chemicals to and from Heysham, with other traffic to and from Northern Ireland and coal and general freight for Lancaster. Most of these workings were with loose-coupled or partly-fitted freight trains, but one exception was the 'Lodger'—a fully-fitted freight from Heysham to Leeds. There were also occasional specials.

Coal trains were numerous enough to require at least three complete trains of empties, one at 2.20am to Monkton Main, the Manvers empties at 10.50am, and, if I remember correctly, one to Snydale. Almost all these duties, whether starting from Heysham or Lancaster, were relieved at Skipton, where, after a break of about half an hour, the enginemen manned a train from Leeds returning to Lancaster or Heysham. Freight working over the LNW section was confined almost entirely to specials from Heysham, one example being a fairly regular turn worked as far as Preston, bound for Tunstead ICI sidings with a load of nitro-chalk.

On the passenger side the workings were a little more extensive. Locally, due to the change in electrification, the service from Lancaster Castle and Green Ayre to Morecambe Promenade and Heysham was worked by a push-and-pull set. The LNW Morecambe trains were worked as a somewhat intermittent shuttle service; they included a couple of turns to Preston, on one of which the locomotive returned with the Manchester–Heysham boat train. There was also a duty which involved the working of Morecambe–Euston through coaches, which were attached to an up main-line train at Castle Station.

One through-working to Crewe and back completed the regular duties on the LNW side. From time to time Green Ayre provided an assisting engine for a south-bound express from Lancaster Castle to Crewe, and during the summer the shed had a turn to Barrow and also worked a duty from Morecambe Euston Road to Ulverston and up the Windermere Lakeside branch, returning to Lancaster with a Blackpool train. In addi-

Compound 4–4–0 No 41081 and 'Crab' 2-6-0 No 42895 on Lancaster shed, 1952 *W. Rickerby*

Lancaster Green Ayre Motive Power Depot
44756 41045 42136 44105 *W. Rickerby*

The 14.55 Heysham–Leeds–Stourton fast goods at Scale Hall headed by Ivatt Class 4 2–6–0 No 43035 *Ian S. Pearsall*

Class 4F 0–6–0s at Sellafield in 1964; a Barrow–Egremart goods headed by No 44377 and a Sellafield–Moor Row workers train with No 44065 *Derek Cross*

Class 4F 0–6–0 No 43931 on the 14.55 Heysham–Leeds goods at Clapham in April 1958 *A. W. H. Pearsall*

Tall chimney Class 4F 0–6–0 No 44403 on a northbound pickup goods, pauses to collect empty wagons from Knighton Fields Coal Wharf sidings, Leicester in March 1957 *A. F. Taylor*

Cab-end view of Class 3F 0–6–0 43583 at Bow Works *M. F. Higson*

An up stopping freight train passing Dillicar behind Class 3F Johnson (reboilered Fowler) 0–6–0 No 43585 in May 1952 *E. D. Bruton*

tion to these turns, Green Ayre also was responsible for working the 'Ulster Express' over its short run between Heysham Harbour and Morecambe Promenade. On the Midland side the passenger workings included the morning 'Residential Express' from Morecambe to Bradford and Leeds, the boat trains from Heysham to Leeds and back, and slow trains to and from Leeds and Bradford. This, then, was the basic pattern of the duties performed by Green Ayre men. Motive power for these various duties was quite varied, and a typical Green Ayre allocation was as follows (some with BR numbers and the others with their previous LMSR numbers).

LMR Class 2P 4–4–0 40362
LMR Class 4P 4–4–0 41045/65/81, 1107/36/52/96/97
LMR Class 2P 0–4–4T 41900–04
LMR Class 4MT 2–6–4T 42135/36, 2589
LMR Class 5MT 2–6–0 42893/95, 2928
LMR Class 4MT 2–6–0 43034/35
LMR Class 3F 0–6–0 43271, 43330
LMR Class 4F 0–6–0 43890, 3984, 4032
LMR Class 2MT 2–6–0 46441
LMR Class 3F 0–6–0– 47381, 7468/69/70/71, 7532, 7639, 7201
LMR Class 8F 2–8–0 48261/86, 8342, 8505
BR Class 2MT 2–6–0 78031

The 3F 0–6–0 tanks worked the Heysham Harbour duties, the Castle shunt and banker, Ladies' Walk and New Zealand shunts, and some trip duties. No 47201 was specially retained on work near the shed; as it had only one injector and a non-functioning pump, duties farther afield would have been too much of a risk. Nos 47468-71 had screw reverse, and were most useful on the Castle banker, or working the 'Ulster Express' from Heysham Harbour to Morecambe Promenade. No 47639 had no vacuum brake, and was usually kept as a spare or trip-engine. The 3F 0–6–0 goods engines were mainly employed on trip-work and of the 4Fs one was allocated to the Quay-shunt duty and one to the Moss-sidings shunt.

The ballast engine for the LNW section was usually No 40362, which until the advent of No 78031 also working the Engineer's Saloon. The Midland section ballast train had whatever engine was spare, usually a 4F 0–6–0 (either a Green Ayre engine or one from another depot), or sometimes a 'Crab' 2–6–0 or an Austerity 2–8–0. Class 2MT 2–6–0 No 46441 had sole command of the Bentham pick-up, usually relieved when under repair by a 3F or 4F 0–6–0. Main-line freight duties were powered chiefly by 'Crab' 2–6–0s and 8F 2–8–0s.

The Green Ayre 8F 2–8–0s worked turn-and-turn about with those from Holbeck, Stourton and Normanton. 4MT Nos 43034/5 were allocated specially to the Leeds Lodger which Lancaster men worked throughout. On rare occasions Fowler and ex LNWR 0–8–0s appeared, together with 3F 0–6–0s from as far away as Derby and Saltley.

The push-and-pull turns provided work for most of the 419XX 0–4–4 tanks, one appearing from time to time on the Lancaster Castle–Morecambe Euston Road duty, while the 2–6–4 tanks worked the principal duties on this branch together with the two turns to Preston; during the summer one was responsible for the Windermere Lakeside turn. Compound 4–4–0s handled the bulk of the Leeds line passenger duties, with the exception of the 'Residential Express', which was hauled by a Class 5 or 5X 4–6–0 from Holbeck shed.

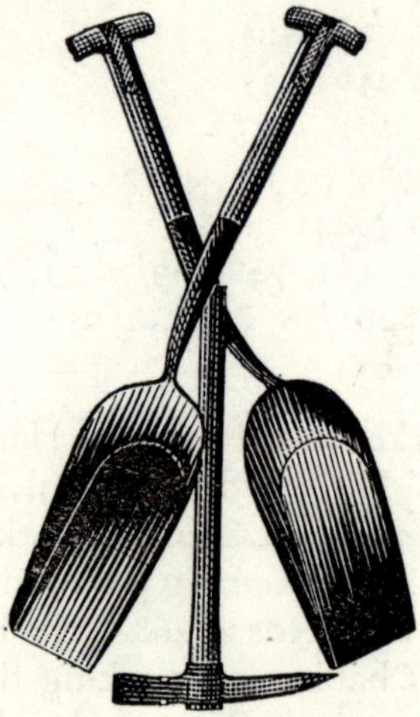

2

First Footplate Experiences

My first turn of duty as a fireman was on the Ladies' Walk shunt-engine (No 47532); it was on night shift and rather a nightmare. I still hadn't solved the injector problem and found great difficulty in getting it to work. When I did get it to work, it was only with considerable wastage and a frequent tendency to 'fly-off'. Gradually the boiler water-level dropped to a very dangerous point and disaster was narrowly averted with some assistance from the driver, who obviously disliked 'green' hands.

That first night seemed 24 hours long. The noise appeared to be deafening and I was extremely glad when suppertime arrived and I was able quietly to take stock in my own dark corner of the cab. We must have shunted solidly for something like three hours; I seemed to have been shovelling continuously and the fire looked very uneven. The water was well down and the injector was sighing, gurgling and slowly—very slowly—topping up the boiler. My mate grunted a few uncharitable comments and then rolled off to the shunters' cabin, probably to have a rest from shunting and calm his nerves sufficiently to climb back on board with me. I took down the rake and levelled the fire a bit, shut off the feed and let the engine get a little more steam. The glow from the fire glinted on the back of the cab and reflected somewhat dully on the firebox back-plate. The gauge lamp had become somewhat choked and had acquired a thick layer of soot in the top of the container.

Burning my already sore fingers, I managed to knock most of the soot out and obtain a somewhat better light. My hands and wrists were both burned, as the result of my trying to fire during a rough shunt and steadying myself on the hot copper pipes! The wrist and lower arm burns had been acquired on the baffle-plate when I was trying to get the coal into the back corners of the box. The reflection of my face in the round port-hole windows, with streaks of sweat staining forehead and cheeks, resembled that of a miner. I had torn my jacket pocket with the shovel handle and my sandwiches had rolled into the oil-box, the lid of which should have provided a seat but had been wrenched off. The cab floor was generously covered with lumps of coal, much of which had fallen off the shovel in my vain attempts to steer it into the firehole when colliding at 10mph with a raft of wagons.

Suddenly I felt very lonely and miserable. Why had I gone through so much to get on to the footplate? If this was a sample of the life, I felt I had been deceived. Hearty laughter came over the night air from the near-by cabin and I could just imagine why; no doubt that so-and-so of a driver was telling the shunters what a buffoon he had for a mate. "Didn't know which end of the shovel to use"; "Ha Ha"; "Keeps falling over his feet"; "Ho Ho"; "Engine would explode if it wasn't for me—didn't teach 'em a thing"; and so on *ad nauseam*.

Away across the yard was a row of friendly little houses where everyone was fast asleep, warm and snug, after doing a clean and sensible daytime job; here was I all alone in a miserable, pale, gas-lit goods yard, with just a few rats for company. Where was the glamour? How on earth had I fallen into this occupation? What in heaven's name made me love engines? I felt very chilly. The fire had burned low, so, forgetting my misery, I livened it up, had a wash in the shovel and sat down and ate my sandwiches.

Work resumed with a vengeance, or so it seemed. The old 'Crab' had revitalised himself and, as keen as mustard, seemed to be hitting wagons left, right and centre. Very gradually the cold light of dawn crept over the yard and tiredness descended on me. I yawned and felt awfully cold. I longed for a good hot cup of tea and bed, and happily, just when I felt I must go to sleep, our to-and-fro movement was checked and I realised that we had been released and sent back to the shed. Thank goodness it was over! I couldn't get out of the shed fast enough.

Somehow I settled down, slowly mastering the injector and becoming more used to firing, while covering an increasingly wide range of duties. The trip between Green Ayre and Castle Station was quite a thrilling short haul. The steep grade linking the two stations had to be stormed from start to finish, and the 3F 0–6–0, sometimes assisted from the rear, would roar away up the bank absolutely all-out, only too often to be stopped by signal outside Castle Station, still on the bank. If this happened, we might be quite unable to move, and the yard pilot would have to come to the rescue. On the other side of Castle Station a similarly steep incline connects the quay with the Glasson branch. The locomotive on this duty was always a 4F 0–6–0, which sometimes had to work 40 or more vans up to the Castle Yards. This feat could be accomplished only by taking a lengthy run at the bank, combined with a really hot fire. Incredible as it may seem, all this effort was frequently wasted by the signalman at Lancaster No 3 box, who refused to accept us at the bank top. On wet or drizzly days this often meant a retreat to the bottom and a fresh start. To gain access to the Castle

Yards this train had to pass the station over the down platform road, a reasonable interval was therefore required to clear the Quay trip. The old stalwart on this job was No 44032, half as strong again as any other known 4F 0–6–0. Sad was the day when she left for Stoke, and woeful was the future. Nos 43890 and 43984 never shone as did No 44032 and they frequently stalled half-way up the bank.

The Quay trip-engine was also responsible for the infrequent runs to Glasson Dock, very often to pick up just one van. This branch resembled part of the erstwhile Colonel Stephens empire, with hedges and trees dangerously overhanging the right-of-way and sleepers in places gradually sinking and rotting. Broken-down fences and dilapidated huts completed the picture with the rather miserable flats and mudbanks of the River Lune as a backcloth. As already mentioned, the Castle Yard-shunter dealt with all LNW traffic and also undertook banking when necessary. To be a little more precise, it was expected to provide banking assistance when required, but most of the crews disliked this time-absorbing task and tried to hide the engine behind vans in an attempt to discourage the practice. Some through southbound freights did not make much effort in climbing the bank, feeling assured that, even if the worst happened, the yard-shunter could be relied upon to 'dig them out'. In some cases, trains booked for banking proved quite able to climb the bank unaided. One of these trains, the up night 'Postal', frequently sneaked away from the banker before the run was half over, sometimes by as much as two carriage-lengths, with 12 or 13 on, and a Princess Pacific!

To be fair, however, the 1 in 100 bank was a severe task from a dead stand and in the autumn leaves falling from the large number of trees on the bank could make it a killer for many southbound freights. The banker, however, could save much time over this section, for some unassisted train could take 20min and more to clear the top. Time intervals on this section were so short that sometimes there was not time for the freights safely to make Oubeck loop ahead of the next up main-line train. In that case the freight might be stopped at Lancaster No 1, at the top of the bank, and backed into the Old yard.

On some occasions when I was working on main-line trains, I wished we had taken banking assistance. One damp misty night we had a full load of nitro-chalk and a Fowler 2–6–0 which not only almost slipped to a standstill but failed with both injectors at the same time. We succeeded in entering the loop at Oubeck with no water visible in the glass and expecting the fusible plug to fail at any minute.

The transition from shunting to more regular main-line work usually accelerated with the approach of summer and the attendant annual holidays. Passed firemen and passed cleaners filled in for regular crews on leave, and the long dull periods of shunting and trip work were temporarily over. Inevitably the reduced skill had some effect on the general performance, but on the whole matters proceeded quite well. Additional seasonal duties also absorbed extra men. Among these duties were the Windermere Lakeside trains. For me such duties were rather a problem. For motive power we had taper-boiler 2–6–4 tanks, and the run involved working from Morecambe Euston Road to Ulverston, where we uncoupled, ran round the train, reversed and made for the Lakeside branch.

The difficulties for me always took place on the latter. The trouble was twofold—keeping the injectors working and picking up the tablets on the single-line section. The slight brake application on nearing the tablet exchange points was always just enough to make the injector blow back. This was specially worrying for two reasons; steam would suddenly envelop the engine, making it difficult for me to see the tablet hoops, and I always feared that the scalding overflow might injure the signalman with whom the tablet was being exchanged, particularly at one place where the point of exchange was down at rail level. On one occasion in particular I got into trouble. Because of the heavy gradients on the branch the water-level in the boiler had dropped to so dangerous a level as to be out of sight as we approached Lakeside station. I was so anxiously trying to get the injector on again that I quite forgot to hand the tablet over at the platform end and so had quite a long walk to give it up.

For compensation, however, the Lakeside turn had quite a lot to offer. The line itself is one of the most beautiful I ever worked over, with a wonderful change of scenery from near sea-level through woods and rock cuttings to the climax at Lakeside, a pretty little terminal station, providing direct exchange with the lake steamers and commanding a fine view. Once at Lakeside there was a long inactive spell before returning with a Blackpool train, usually worked by a Class 5 4–6–0 from that shed. Blackpool engines on this turn were usually well turned out, very clean and supplied with good grade I coal—huge slabs of the best Yorkshire. To Ulverston the engine ran tender-first and it was quite a thrill to pound out of Lakeside up through the stone cuttings, blasting showers of cinders high into the surrounding trees, and with no injector troubles. The run from Ulverston to Lancaster, stopping at Grange-over-Sands and Carnforth, was an added thrill as quite a turn of speed could be attained.

Grange-over-Sands was a test for a young fireman and woe betide him if there was any sign of smoke. A continuous watch was kept by the local Railway Vigilante Society, which made regular complaints at the slightest sign of a 'dirty' chimney. Safety-valves also had to be controlled, if only to pacify the tame-duck population in the park adjoining the railway. One cannot leave the Lakeside branch without mentioning the dye-works at Greenodd. All the houses, trees and the like, for some distance around, were liberally coated in a thick shroud of blue dust—as were the workers, who provided an almost uncanny sight. It is said, locally, that the dye is so good that it has even penetrated the water supply, hence the blue population!

Ulverston is only a short run from Barrow and we had one turn in summer through to Barrow. Apart from the famed Lindal bank and a very tight tunnel at Dalton, this run provided little else of note, other than skirting Morecambe Bay and, the chance occasionally to see the most beautiful sunsets, for Morecambe Bay sunsets (and shrimps!) are second to none and a truly wonderful sight.

To get to know the lines around Lancaster there was no better way than to fire the Engineer's train, either with his saloon or on the ballasting duties. The Lancaster Engineer had his own regular driver, Johnny Bayman, a short, rather wizened little man, with the nicest temperament you could possibly wish for. Johnny had the job for years and had an astonishingly good knowledge of most lines in north-west England. Some lines he rarely ran over more than once a year, but this did not deter him at all, and it was said he could run over any road with but one trip; he also knew the road as far as Stafford and Hereford, as well as the surrounding lines in the north-west. The Engineer's Department also had a regular guard with an equally wide knowledge of the more remote lines.

The saloon itself was housed in the Engineer's Yard (off the Quay branch) in its own special shed, and collecting the saloon preparatory to going on a run was something of a ritual. Extreme care in coupling-up and moving the saloon was the requirement and, indeed, from the care exercised at stopping and during running that we observed we might have been working the Royal Train. The saloon attendant who prepared and served meals on a run would give messages from time to time, indicating when soup was likely to be served, so that extra caution might be observed. In spite of all our care, however, it was not uncommon during stops for a worried face to appear at the engine, reprimanding us for a particularly severe lurch or a too sudden stop.

One typical run to Carlisle I remember, with the then new Engineer's engine No 78031, on which we stopped to inspect various bridges and culverts, with intermittent sprints to avoid expresses. The return was nonstop and a highly exciting descent of Shap was the reward for a not particularly strenuous day.

When not actually working the saloon, ballast work up and down the line—usually between Preston and Carnforth—was the usual routine with trips down what was left of the Garstang & Knott End (memorable on one occasion for the near slaughter of numerous chickens), the Glasson

Dock branch and the ballast tip at Heysham. The ballast train Headquarters was situated at the one-time terminus of the Lancaster & Preston Junction Railway, in the Old Yard situated almost at the top of the 1 in 100 bank south of Lancaster Castle. On one occasion we were ordered to proceed light engine to Heysham tip, to bring a raft of empty ballast wagons back to the Old Yard ready for week-end ballasting operations. The engine was 2P 4–4–0, No 40362, and the 40 or so empties proved too much for her adhesion. It was quite a struggle to get from Heysham to Morecambe Promenade, where we had to run round the train. The incline from Bare Lane to South Junction almost found us stalled, straddling the West Coast main line. The end to this six-mile epic struggle took place on the celebrated bank out of Lancaster, where we finally expired under a shower of smoke and cinders to await the ever-reluctant banker!

No 40362 and I were concerned in several other quite different affairs, one an 18-hour stint on the reballasting of the mainline near Garstang, after severe flooding. There we were, in a most exposed position, in biting wind and driving rain, without food or warm drink, and fighting with a tarpaulin which persistently broke loose to become a sail rather than a shield for us from the elements. As usual, Johnny Bayman was the driver, and through all this the poor little soul sat huddled in his thick overcoat, without as much as the top of his head showing, gently moving a wagon length about every three-quarters of an hour. Food supplies ran out, owing to our having underestimated the extent of the job. Some six train-loads of ballast from Shap were sent to remake the line, which had exchanged the ballast chips for mangolds from an adjoining field. The flooding had been caused by a fallen tree blocking a river underbridge. Gales and persistent rain caused the water to wash out large sections of the track formation. On another occasion with No 40362, hauling one open wagon and a brake-van, we emptied signalbox dustbins in and around Preston, one of the most menial duties that I ever performed.

Ballast duties were quite important in the Lancaster roster sheets, and frequently men were booked week in and week out for both Midland and North Western ballast work. As previously stated, the Midland duties were to Clapham and the old Midland and Furness Joint line from Wennington to Carnforth, as well as to Morecambe Promenade and Heysham. The Wennington–Carnforth line was very rural, with an abundance of wild-life —foxes, rabbits, stoats and weasels—and thanks to the pheasants and other game birds, the resident staff on the line were said to live particularly well! Almost the only thing I can remember acquiring on this line, however, was a tender-load of holly with berries one Christmas-time. At one time rabbits were a regular 'perk' for engine-crews, but mixamatosis put an end to that. The only other catch I ever saw was a number of salmon 'rescued' from the River Lune during the summer months, when drought had reduced the river to a trickle and had left many large fish stranded. After all, with time to spare on the local 'pick-up' it was the least one could do for the poor things!

Green Ayre depended largely on freight—coal from Yorkshire, traffic to and from Ireland, the combined products of ICI and Shell from Heysham, trains of ammonia tanks ('snowballs', as they were known locally, owing to the frost incrustations on the tank barrels), nitro-chalk, diesel oil and petrol. The tank trains were all heavy, and were usually worked by 8F 2–8–0s. On one occasion I remember firing on an oil train to Skipton with a young passed fireman as a mate. It was on a winter's night, and about half-way to Clapham we encountered a thick snowstorm. We had topped Clapham at a good pace and as usual had cracked a few jokes at having had a clear run without any troubles. Whether it was the snow or the dense blackness of the night I shall never know, but somehow we completely misjudged our position and found ourselves pounding down towards Settle Junction with our load of oil and the signals against us. Brakes hard on made no apparent difference, and even with the able assistance of our guard, indicated by showers of sparks from the brake-van, we were unable to hold the train. As a last despairing effort, we put the engine flat-out into reverse and, opening out the whistle, screamed 'pops' on it to attract the Junction-box. Roaring, banging and crashing, and when we were barely half a mile away from the Junction, the signal changed to green and we could breathe again. So desperate had been our efforts that I was quite unable to release the handbrake till we had stopped and with the coal-hammer had duly persuaded it to act.

Coal empties figured three times daily and one of them, destined for Monkton Main Collieries, departed from Ladies' Walk siding at the glorious hour of 2.20am. It always intrigued me that anyone should be so desperate as to require coal empties to be despatched at that unearthly hour. Anyway, I performed on this little excursion on several occasions. The trouble with this job, apart from the hours, was the number of empties—usually a full train—and the 4F 0–6–0 employed thereon. Other handicaps included a fairly high proportion of wagons with grease axle-boxes and guards who were more anxious to attend to their brake-van fires than to ensure that all handbrakes were released. The 18 or so miles to Clapham were quite hard enough without any extra resistance, and on several occasions, when the going had been exceptionally hard, we stopped at Bentham, ostensibly for water but also to release anything up to six handbrakes and, on one occasion, actually to release the guard's handbrake.

The question of guards and handbrakes was always a bone of contention between the 'front end' and the 'rear'. Guards fall into numerous classes by enginemens standards—good, bad and indescribable. The older guards, on the whole, were first-rate men, always doing their utmost to ensure that a train was in the best order for the 'front-end' men. Some of the younger element, however, were rather obnoxious characters, who took a delight in taking a rise out of the enginemen on every possible occasion. In consequence every good engineman vowed to 'wrap the so-and-so round his own handbrake' by roughing up a trip to such an extent that these trouble-makers either mended their ways or found other jobs. I recall one particular guard, a young chap in his twenties, who most decidedly knew the lot. He knew so much, indeed, that when we had to marshal a train it always took twice as long with him as without him. This individual so persistently aggravated the engine-crews that his very life was at stake with some of them, and I believe he received some particularly rough trips, including many bruises, before he calmed down somewhat.

Some guards, like a few drivers, are of the nervous type, who apply the handbrake even before the train is over the hill. On one occasion we were nearing Clapham and noticed that the van handbrake was on and that sparks were flying from the wheels. So we stopped the train and just waited. In due course the guard appeared, demanding to know when we might have enough steam to re-start. We replied that re-starting depended on his quick release of his handbrake, whereupon after some argument he retired defeated to his van and we were able to resume our journey. Great care had to be taken, however, as some of the more miserable 'brake-rats' would book lost time at the least opportunity, and while we could usually provide a reason for delays, it was a nuisance to have to fill up reports.

I had many struggles up to Clapham with trains of empties, always on 4F 0–6–0s and usually covering the surrounding countryside with dense clouds of black smoke, gradually mortgaging the water in the boiler, with the firebox door firmly closed and fire-irons frequently in use. It was no fun flogging the empties for mile after mile on a rising gradient, half asleep and sometimes in driving rain with a sick engine, and with the contents of a Derby cab-roof gutter pouring over one's back and down one's neck. Yet I wish I could do it all over again!

Coming up the other side, from Skipton, it was just as much fun. Very often we were put inside at Delaney's Sidings, and a more desperate place from which to re-start I cannot imagine. We had to pull out of Delaney's on a reverse curve, straight on to a stiff bank at 1 in 132–165. The constant procession of trains out of the siding had made the exit extremely slippery, and a driver's hell. Once we took twenty-five minutes to get out of Delaney's, and then only succeeded because I shovelled dirt on to the rails for what seemed miles.

Many times we crawled out of Delaney's to the accompaniment of a torrent of curses, slipping, shuddering and sliding, with a steady column of black smoke shooting skywards and the throaty bark of our 4F fighting desperately through Gargrave and Bell Busk to the summit just short of Hellifield, after which a final burst of action down the falling gradient to Settle Junction would enable us to storm Giggleswick bank and coast home. Many a time it was touch-and-go with no more than 140lb of steam on the clock, an inch of water in the gauge-glass, spluttering injectors and a grade of coal that never seemed to burn. One glorious exit from Delaney's brought half the brick arch down and only very hard labour with the fire-irons brought us into Hellifield at all!

Strangely enough, my finest trip over this line was with a 4F 0-6-0 hauling a twenty-coach empty stock train which we took over at Skipton to work through to Morecambe. No 44207, one of the tall-chimney 4Fs from Holbeck shed, with exhaust injector, pounded her way from Skipton up to Clapham without any fuss at all.

To experience the excitements of this line at their maximum was to view the antics of the excursion trains to Morecambe on a summer Saturday. Numerous trains had to be worked from Leeds and Bradford, mainly powered by particularly indifferent machines, grubbed up from their usual trip work, and all trying, often in vain, not to lose more than half an hour on schedule, or so it seemed. If these engines were reluctant to get to Morecambe, they were even more reluctant to go home, and for this reason we had to station two stand-bys, one at Morecambe and the other at Bentham at the height of the season. Some of the evening excursions to see the illuminations would have engines booked to return almost immediately with an earlier day excursion. It so happened that one weekend I was on No 41107, standby at Morecambe, detailed to take a returning excursion to Bradford; the incoming booked engine and crew with the illuminations special had lost over half an hour, and was not likely to arrive at Morecambe until the balance job by rights should be near Bentham. We had twelve non-corridor coaches and had a wonderful run to Bradford. We passed the other engine, with its crew examining their stationary mount, near Green Ayre station, and some ferocious-looking passengers hanging out of the windows of the non-corridor coaches!

These excursions were amusing for another reason. Some of the crews booked off at Morecambe for several hours, and duly came to work with suitable seaside attire underneath their overalls. To see some of these stalwarts, dirty, dishevelled and quite worn out, nursing a sickly engine into Morecambe, instead of being ready for the 'Prom' was quite a joke. These engines were all looked after by one or two sets of men from Lancaster, who tended fires and boilers, but sometimes the tending ones were not so tending, and a fire would go out! Then followed scurrying to find old sleepers and firewood, oil and paraffin to get a fire up quickly, when the panic and perspiration were quite as amusing as the best music-hall turn.

Morecambe engine yard on a summer Saturday night might hold 12 to 15 engines—perhaps more; sometimes a whole works outing, such as that of the Raleigh Bicycle Works of Nottingham, would descend on us, and such a large assembly would require very careful attention and location to ensure that no delay ensued when each engine was required for the return workings. Turmoil of this kind demanded a shed deputy-foreman in control, and this little sub-depot of Green Ayre then became larger than the parent depot. All manner of machines would appear on excursions, 3Fs, 4Fs, 5s, 5Xs, 2Ps, compounds, 3Ps, Bls and others. To see the best side of the picture was to be on the stand-by duty at Bentham, observing the antics of crews—burned by the sun and ailing perhaps from seaside headaches—force some very reluctant engines past, amid clouds of smoke and cinders, with their human cargo swallowing bottled beer, wearing funny hats and flying streamers. A delightful contrast indeed! Many of these specials that found the going too hard resorted to water column tactics at Bentham, and fortified both tender and boiler before resuming the attack on to Clapham.

Mechanical ailments were not uncommon and their sufferers were hurried to Green Ayre for fitters' attention. Most of the troubles were cured sufficiently to enable the engines to return home, but some were incapable of return without more drastic attention, when the pitifully small reserve of Lancaster motive power would have to come to the rescue. Some Yorkshire crews found cold comfort from the exchange and the pressure would build up at Bentham, from which the stand-by would assist a reluctant Green Ayre 'hero' to wheeze away to Clapham.

The reader will doubtless have noted the author's rather disparaging comments on the ubiquitous 4F 0–6–s. No other locomotive, perhaps with the exception of the LNW 0–8–0s, created so much discussion among crews of the sheds that I knew. To some a 4F was a masterly machine capable of being handled by two-year-olds, and able to pull a house down. Others, particularly LNW line men, despised the 4F and regarded it as a very poor tool. For myself, I noted subtle differences in the class as a whole. The best engines were Derby-built, and in particular Midland-built. All 4Fs with the taller chimneys (blue circles on the cab sides) seemed good steamers. On the other hand the 445XX series and Horwich-maintained engines were often poor machines compared with the earlier series and the Derby-maintained engines.

The major problem with a 4F was steam; it would either steam or it would not. The steam troubles were, I think, due mainly to the rather sharp inclination of the grate. Coal would not stop under the door and would not burn in any quantity under the arch. A 4F needed good coal, more so than other engines, and also a clean boiler. Midland Railway type parallel boilers seemed very susceptible to scaling and the method of feed to the boiler was particularly cooling, not like the top-feed type on taper boilers. Smokebox doors leaked, as the method of fastening was not very good, and insufficient blast, especially at low average goods train speeds, did not help combustion. The auxiliaries on a Midland type boiler absorbed a good deal of steam, and use of the jet, could not be afforded to any great extent. The large ejector was a colossal drain on the boiler and was only used when starting or stopping, or when the boiler was so low in steam that the brakes were dragging. Compared with the 3F, the boiler of a 4F was not in the same class. In fact, if only the 3F had had more adhesive weight it could have licked a 4F any day. A 3F could be worked heavily with both injectors on, if needs be, a feat that I never managed with a 4F 0–6–0.

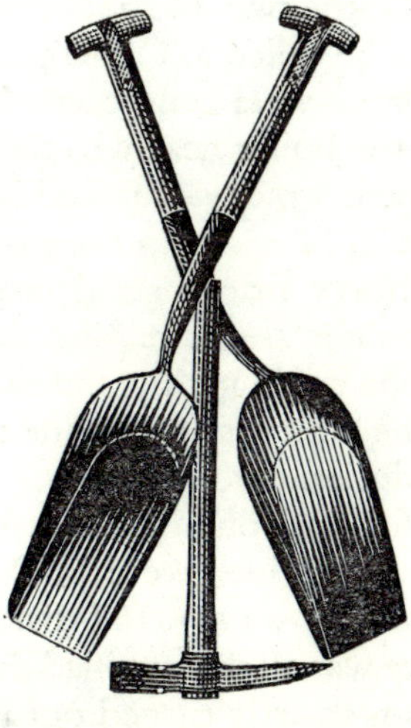

3

Some Lancaster Drivers

During the time I was at Lancaster, 4F 0–6–0s Nos 43890 and 43984 were never regarded as main-line engines. Most of the main-line work performed by this class on the Heysham to Hellifield section was by engines stationed at Stourton (Leeds) and Skipton, with occasional examples from Normanton, Royston and Hellifield. The Lancaster 'twins' were employed on the Quay shunt and on trip work to and from Moss Sidings. Frankly they were barely fit for even this sort of work; neither engine would steam freely, though while they were engaged only on local work this did not really matter very much. Of the two, No 43890 was decidedly the worst. If any engine was entitled to be called a 'Camel', this was it! The trips from Green Ayre to Moss Sidings were only carried out with this engine by mortgaging the water in the boiler nearly to the lead-plug limit. As soon as the regulator was opened, a race developed between the needle on the pressure-gauge and the level of water in the glass, as to which could fall the faster. Light firing, heavy firing, good coal, bad coal—it made no difference, No 43890 was not a 'steam' engine. As long as local work only was involved, however, one could get by, but during the summer months the line was stretched to the limit for power, and the 'twins' would be commandeered for main-line duties.

By the greatest of misfortune, one of Lancaster's lowliest firemen and one of Lancaster's lowliest engines were booked to perform together, and from the start things went wrong. If I disliked No 43890, I disliked her driver even more. Here was all that typified the old Midland Railway to me. A great hulk of a man, smartly turned out in a white shirt and black tie, with that wretched little wyvern (seemingly enjoying a secret joke) set high in the front of his cap, this so-and-so made no bones about his dislike for young-hand firemen. He had absolutely no time for them, and with his usual attitude he made a good deal of fuss about me as a mate, until he discovered that owing to his regular fireman not turning up there was nobody else. We had met once before and an instant dislike set in. between us. Every remark was a command, snapped and snarled with great contempt. His whole attitude was one of sheer disgust. The Midland would never have tolerated the passed-cleaner of today—and he still wouldn't. Furthermore, firemen were there to do a job, and if they couldn't manage it or were in trouble, that was just too bad. So be it, here I was with No 43890, bless her rotten boiler, a hell of a mate and a full train of empties to take to Skipton.

For some time the coal supply at Lancaster had been mainly Wigan 'blind'. The term 'blind' I assumed was because of the apparent absence of coal; not a piece was in sight, nothing more than a grey slaty mess of slack. The fire was a delicious shade of purple-blue, and despite efforts with the dart and pricker, it did not improve very much by being knocked about. With some terrier action in the tender I managed to locate a few forgotten lumps in the vicinity of the tank filler, and with these for encouragement under the door and a few shots down the sides, I closed the doors a little, gave a turn on the blower and hoped for the best.

His Highness arrived a few minutes before we were due off and without even a grunt from him we dropped down to the yard for our train. By some miracle, by the time we were hooked up and the lamps had been adjusted, the safety-valves blew and with that we got the 'right-away'. I had decided that the only way to get to Skipton was by firing 'little and often', and with a whole lot of praying. About half-a-mile out, when passing the power-station on the way to Halton, I gave her another six or so shovelsful and hopefully put the injector on, and that did it. Back went the needle! By the bottom of Halton Bank (a mile of 1 in 132), and with pressure still dropping, I shut the injector off. We had been wasting no time and had made a run for the bank; I had let the damper stay full open and boxed up the doors; but somehow she just would not have it. We topped the bank and went through Caton with three-quarters of a glass and I think about 160lb on the clock. By Claughton Manor brick works, and running almost on the level, things hadn't improved much and the boiler had got well down. On went the injector after another sharp round, but somehow the smoke just would not clear; a thick black treacly cloud poured out of the chimney, and that was about the only response. By Wennington we were down to 140lb and half a glass.

My companion deigned to observe the situation by swinging his bulk away from his cab side for a momentary grunt, and swung back. I decided to use the pricker on the fire! Somehow she had to liven up a bit. Three or four pulls through, and the doors slammed to—again with no response. Things were in a mess and I could not do anything more. At Low Bentham, with 120lb of steam and water in the bottom nut, I put the feed on again. A blow-up was inevitable. The large frame of my mate was still angled out of the cab, completely indifferent to what was going on. I could have wept as gradually we lost speed and finally, with a despairing chug, ground to a stop. Now there was a response from the other side of the cab. Slowly he straightened up, closed the regulator, wound on the handbrake and glowered. With a sneer, he said 'When you are ready, I will start again.'

The fire was anything but hot, in fact it was rather blue and clinkery; the brick arch was only just glowing, and there just did not seem to be any remedy. Somehow I coaxed her to '160' and half-a-glass, and so, still without any consultation, the right-hand member of our crew started away. Three miles farther on we gasped to a standstill once again. The fire was worse and it took still longer to gain some steam. Things were now so bad that I knew we could not make Hellifield, let alone Skipton, without further stops. Despairingly I asked my glowering companion to have us put in to the siding at Clapham so that I could clean the fire a bit. He did not even reply, but stopped the engine in Clapham Station with water out of sight in the gauge-glass and a blue mass in the box. Scouring the tender for lumps, I knocked the fire about and put the jet hard on. I tested the smokebox, but that was all right. Only half ready, we set off again. If only we could reach the top of the mile at 1 in 100 beyond Eldroth box, I thought we might make it to Hellifield.

But it was not to be; the engine got over the top but the train did not and we stuck yet once again. It is hard to convey my feelings at the time. I just felt too sick to care any more. The fire was as dead as anything and gradually getting deeper and deeper. Somehow we pulled the train over the summit and coasted down to Settle Junction. Not a pound of steam was gained, however, and we gave up altogether between there and Long Preston, to which point a Hellifield engine came and dragged us into Hellifield.

The worst, however, was yet to come. We had been stuck between Settle Junction and Long Preston for quite a time, and had held up the Carlisle line rather badly. A sort of miniature inquiry started on the platform at Hellifield, with the glowering one acting as the main speaker. He just could not condemn me enough. I had stopped the whole line, delayed everything from Carlisle to Leeds, I should not be allowed on the footplate at all and I should probably get paid up—I certainly ought to be. Back at Lancaster he started again. I just left him to get on with it, and miserably made my way home.

In defence I said that the coal was awful, and the fire was not in proper order to start with. A quick retort was to the effect that I should have said so before we started, but that was no good now. Looking back on this sad day, I doubt if I could have improved matters much. We were short of engines and supplied with terrible coal. I believe that No 43890's boiler

View of yards, east of Lancaster Green Ayre. New Zealand sidings are in the far left background and 'Crab' 2–6–0 No 42895 is marshalling a train in Ladies Walk sidings *A. W. H. Pearsall*

Class 2P 4–4–0 No 40332 waiting to leave Birmingham New Street on the 17.45 stopping train to Bristol in April 1957 *M. Mensing*

A Leeds–Morecambe train leaving Leeds behind Compound 4–4–0 No 41080

E. Treacy

Class 3F 0–6–0T No 47381 on trip work between Lancaster and Heysham at Torrisholme

A. W. H Pearsall

Ivatt Class 2 2–6–0 No 46488 *Ronald Wright*

Ivatt Class 2 2–6–0 Nos 46426 and 46458 double-head a special from Leeds, near Troutbeck between Keswick and Penrith in June 1964

A. R. Thompson

was probably coated with scale and that the engine was quite incapable of doing main-line work. Some days after the event, and with better coal (who arranged this?) No 43890 with a footplate inspector misbehaved again—only once, I believe—but showed herself to be nigh on useless.

Some time later I well remember visiting Derby works and seeing the tubes of a 4F boiler being removed. The business was extremely difficult owing to the thick coating of scale on the outside of the tubes. I was most surprised at the time, finding it hard to believe that any heat could have been applied to the water. Naturally my thoughts strayed back to No 43890; I realised that a jemmy in her blast-pipe would have been a 'must' for future main-line canters, and even that would probably not have been enough assistance.

With this one exception I don't think I ever had a mate who didn't try to help me when difficulties developed. Not many months after this run my driver on No 43890 died rather suddenly, not I believe due in any way to this most unfortunate affair. Apart from some of the old top-link men at Crewe, who seemed to have enough to do to pick up their lunch-boxes, let alone a shovel, all other mates were truly mates, encouraging, helping either by firing or pulling coal forward in the tender, or simply making suggestions, and always easing the work on the engine considerably if trouble started.

Next to the Residential express from Morecambe to Bradford and Leeds, working the Barrow–Euston express down to Crewe, was the top job at Lancaster. It was practically the only job on which Jubilee and Royal Scots 4–6–0s could be found and for a young fireman, anxious to experience greater things, firing one of these engines was something to look forward to. On this turn I had my first run on a Jubilee, with No 45603, and I remember it well, for members of the Railway Executive we passengers in the train and an Inspector rode with us to make sure that we kept time. Rather amusingly this gentleman had quite a job that day, as I found great difficulty at first in firing to the front of the box, and the exhaust injector, owing to the extreme roughness of the engine, had to be held in the operating position all the way. Nevertheless, I took to the Crewe duty very quickly, enjoying the run which, with the type of engines we had, was far superior to the slogging matches over the Leeds line. My first Royal Scot run also took place on this job, and I was amazed at the power of these locomotives. No engine previously had given me such a sense of power and ease of working. The climb out of Lancaster Bank could be taken quite in one's stride. The only problem that this job provided was the question of finding one's way around Crewe North shed, a truly enormous one by my standards and extremely easy to get lost in. It was still a problem when I was stationed there later on!

A visit to Horwich one day with No 43034, which we took for shopping, was not without interest. They used visiting crews to take repaired engines light from there to Bolton shed. We had the choice of two—an LYR 0–6–0 or another 430XX 2–6–0. We chose the latter, as on reflection, neither of us had been entertained by the 'Lanky' breed before.

One late summer evening I was called at short notice to assist a London train from Lancaster to Crewe. A compound had been made ready and without more ado we wheeled up to Castle Station and duly attached ourselves. My mate was rather a nervous chap and deep consultation took place as to who should be responsible for the brakes. Despite a very clear rule on the matter such consultations were not infrequent, sometimes at the instigation of the pilot drivers, sometimes at that of the drivers of the train engines. After a little more conferring, and as there was still plenty of light, my mate decided to assume control of the brakes and we set off. The engine was a Manningham one, No 41063 I seem to remember, and performed excellently, giving no steam trouble whatever. We duly arrived at Crewe, dropped on to the North shed, turned and watered, ready for a return job—this time unassisted. We had an hour or so to wait and adjourned to the mess-room for a bite to eat.

During this time a very thick fog had developed and in these circumstances my mate reported that he felt unable to work the train. So I found myself with a strange driver and on a run that I shall never forget. Soon I understood my mate's reluctance to drive. We crept from block to block, and firing became quite secondary to the all-important job of locating signals. To me this task was even more difficult, because of my lack of knowledge of the road. It took us nearly two hours to reach Wigan. Here, the driver's own fireman came up to the engine and, saying he felt certain that I must have had enough, he sent me back into the train to warm up and sleep off some of the strain. I felt a little ashamed, however, and a little frightened. Actions like these might cause us to lose all work over the LNW line.

Lancaster men were more at home on the Preston section and here the Manchester–Heysham boat train was regarded as quite the top assignment. The run was handled by tank engines, specially drafted for the job—Nos 42135/36—which had replaced the compounds, to avoid turning at destination and other problems. The job had a fast timing for a tank engine, 24min for the 21·0 miles from Preston to Lancaster. However, nothing ever runs entirely sweetly, and Nos 42135/36 were not quite up to the work for they would not steam. An Inspector rode the train for some weeks, but without much result. One had to leave Preston with a really hot fire (without smoke or having the safety-valves blowing while standing at Preston), and even then, with their inherent injector troubles and finicky appetite, the engines were difficult. The problem was finally overcome, though not entirely satisfactorily, by ensuring that regardless of the self-cleaning equipment the tubes were regularly blown. Firemen still had to take considerable care with the fire to ensure that sufficient steam was generated. I don't think the big tanks were ever perfect on this run and they continued from time to time to have offdays and to lose time. I only remember doing the job once, and we ran most of the way with about 160lb of steam only and half an inch of water—yet all this time Barrow and Oxenholme men were doing fast runs with tanks and having no trouble at all, but they had Fowler tanks with exhaust injectors. Progress, it seemed, was nil.

The top-link motive power at Lancaster were the compound 4–4–0s. Compounds had been at Lancaster for over 20 years and had replaced 2P and 3P 4–4–0's, on the Leeds and Bradford jobs. For some obscure reason someone regarded them as well suited to our line and every withdrawal was matched by a new arrival. That they gave fairly constant trouble and were not particularly popular may be gathered from the fact that several attempts had been made by the men to obtain different power. However, as long as there was a compound in the country, Green Ayre would be almost certain to receive it in the end. The men had requested Class 5 4–6–0s but the powers-that-be regarded all the Lancaster duties as Class 4 power only, and new engines in any event were rarely supplied to Lancaster.

During my time, the Lancaster compounds, taken as a whole, were not a particularly bright collection. Nos 41107 and 41152 alone were reputable; the remainder varied from average to just hopeless. Without doubt the worst was No 41081, a reject from over the Border, and a consistent terror. She just would not steam and no amount of coaxing would alter this. Fire her thick, thin, hammer her, do what you would, No 41081 was the very devil to handle; No 41136, another ex-Scottish engine, was little better and decidedly rougher. The remainder fell between these standards.

Compounds were in trouble with all manner of crews, top-link or otherwise, and much time was lost, mainly due to poor steaming, but often through constant slipping or, what was even worse, an inability to start. Starting compounds from stations was an art in itself, and I have on several occasions worked from Leeds to Clapham, reversing and rolling back at every station in order to restart, the regulator having to be snatched open, combined with a swift move to full forward gear. Long stretches of running were done with simple propulsion, to keep time, which was another problem, for rarely could the engines find enough steam to meet the constant demand. For rough riding I know no parallel; all our compounds were rough and all seemed springless. Points and crossings were taken in a series of crashes and lurches. This lack of springing caused every nut, bolt and rivet in the cab and footplate to work loose and set up a constant rattle while the engine was on the move.

To fire these creatures without sustaining too much physical injury was a work of art. One of two methods had to be adopted; either one rolled like a drunken sailor with each pitch of the engine, or one wedged oneself firmly against the splasher-cum-seat which projected into the cab, the driver hoisting himself out of the way and sitting side-saddle on top of the wooden box-like top of the reverser and adjusting it as necessary from behind his back. For a Midland Railway engine the compounds had a particularly large and long grate, and required firing mainly under the door and along the sides—in theory. In practice, thanks to their rough riding, one pitched the coal wherever it seemed most likely to burn, and sometimes this would seem to be anywhere but where one actually put it.

A compound was particularly careful as to what it digested, and much of the coal supplied to Green Ayre was anything but suitable. So anxious were the top link men to get better runs, that large quantities of grade 1 coal would be loaded at Holbeck on the tender, in the cab, and even on the back of the tender round the tank filler, to mix in with the Lancaster supply in an endeavour to get better steaming. Some of the Lancaster coals clinkered within 10 to 20 miles and no compound performed well with a dirty fire. The regular crews even resorted to doctoring the blastpipe in an effort to get better steaming. The tubes and boiler were cleaned regularly, but this alone was not enough and trouble with compounds was fairly persistent. Miles of compound running was done with the driver devoting all his free time to opening and shutting the firebox door for his fireman, in an attempt to keep her as 'hot' as possible.

Priming was yet another problem. With much over three-quarters of a glass away they would roar, semi-hydraulic, till they either cleared themselves or, bent their connecting-rods or knocked the cylinder-covers out. Once a compound started to prime, priming rarely ceased till half the boiler had been emptied. Worse still, priming often resulted in water getting into the train brake-pipes and then the whole outfit would gradually grind to a halt. Slipping was another regular trick of the compounds, and sometimes this took place after the regulator had been closed—a sort of delayed action slip. Several cases of side-rods being bent or thrown took place through the sheer violence of this slipping.

On down runs Thackley Tunnel, near Apperley Bridge, was a notorious place for this. The tunnel lining was well and truly perforated and the constant dripping of water in the tunnel made for an extremely slippery rail. With steam hard on until the western end a driver had frequently to close and snatch open his regulator to keep going and avoid the chance of stalling. The volume of noise created by a compound in tunnels, also, was so severe that one often did not realise that the engine had slipped until it was too late. The chimney often gave the first indication—by throwing out a fountain of red-hot coal.

The compounds had sanders, but a locomotive with dry, fully operative sanders was a great rarity, and any sort of aid by sanding could usually be discounted; in general they merely provided a jet of steam which only added to the already slippery conditions. Starting at stations on upgrades (when this feat had been accomplished) could be very tricky, and often three or four slips occurred until one got well under way. Loss of time thus acquired had to be made up by smart inter-station work. Fortunately the compounds were, if nothing else, very free runners and provided you could stand their incessant racket and hang on tight they could usually be relied on to pick up the odd minute.

Most 'local' compounds had one live and one exhaust injector, though some of the earlier series had only live steam injectors. The Midland pattern exhaust injector was a much more finicky piece of equipment than that provided on standard LMS engines, and the poor driver would be constantly regulating the live steam injector—with his foot, if he was operating the fire-doors as well! As with the 3F and 4F 4–4–0s some compounds still had the old Midland type chain-and-flap door, a positive menace on a shy steamer. The fire-irons were very necessary pieces of equipment, the dart and rake in particular, and frequent fire prodding was resorted to.

A compound run of more than usual note occurred early in my footplate career and involved the night boat train from Leeds to Heysham. I had heard sufficient tales about this duty to be more than apprehensive on seeing that it was to be my lot to fire it one evening. Apparently it was somewhat sharply timed and heavily loaded. Only a crack compound and crew could really handle the job successfully. To lose time on this job earned black marks indeed; delay in the boat departure for Northern Ireland was tantamount to criminal negligence.

Many woeful tales were told of the hard struggles encountered by crews endeavouring to maintain time with difficult engines, lack of steam and a host of other troubles. As to this trip, until then, I had had only three duties as far as Leeds, and then nothing more than the rather humble (but to me sufficiently difficult) stopping trains. My mate turned out to be a youngish passed-fireman, who, while cheerful enough and doing his best to be encouraging, obviously had more than enough to do driving the train, without any further possible worry of steam shortage.

The outward stage of the journey was a stopping train to Leeds, where we were due about 7pm. The locomotive concerned was compound No 41136; she was nearly due for shopping (as it turned out later, for scrapping), and violently rough. Practically everything about her rattled, banged and shook. Nothing could adequately describe her state; footplating, cab, doors, tender and numerous backplate fittings vibrated and clattered alarmingly, and points and crossings were something of a nightmare; as with resounding bangs this springless wonder careered over them. Even more unfortunately, she was fired from the right-hand side of the cab. Up till now I had had very little experience of this type of firing and found it exceptionally difficult to propel shovelfuls of coal exactly where I wanted them. Indeed, one out of three never made it and the narrow footplate floor was rapidly filled to a considerable depth with cobbles and slack. When we were in motion the noise created by the rattling and crashing was positively frightening, and made speech quite impossible. Frequently I lost my footing and found myself flung with great force against the sharp edge of the toolbox-cum-seat which flanked my side of the cab.

As far as Bingley things had been just about bearable, but from here to Leeds a non-stop sprint was required, where the true character of our steed really showed up. Frankly, one could do little but hang on tight. If the din had already been bad, it was now twice as much so, and threading Thackley Tunnel I honestly felt that she was falling to bits. Within the confines of this bore the noise was amplified to terrific proportions and I was certain we would leave the rails. Somehow this horror was averted and we continued our headlong run of terror, clattering through Apperley Bridge, Calverley and Rodley at an ever-increasing speed. By this time I had shut my eyes. I revived sufficiently when passing Armley and thankfully stepped on to the platform at Leeds City to recover a little of my shattered senses. Within a few minutes I was back on board her, running light to Holbeck shed for water, a little coal, and to turn. These chores completed, we clanked back to City Station, where we stood on the engine road and had a bite to eat. My mate was noticeably on edge—he had obviously summed up both his engine and his fireman and feared somewhat for the return journey.

Now I was feeling a little better, even though it had not been easy getting to Leeds, and it was likely to be a good deal harder getting back. Having loosened the firebed a little, I took stock of our fuel supply. It was undoubtedly very good but also very large. Massive slabs of best Yorkshire hards firmly wedged the doors, but with considerable difficulty I managed to free a few of the lumps and chipped them into suitable sizes for pushing into the firebox. At this stage my somewhat diminished confidence received a further jolt. My mate was most anxious that we should neither make smoke nor let the safety-valves blow, and so the operation of building up a reasonable fire was held up until about 20min before departure. Incidentally, on looking back, I attribute much of my early trouble on the road to well meaning but ill-advised comment from the opposite side. It was far better to have too much steam at the beginning, for with skill and experience this could soon be controlled, whereas a bad fire at the start always spelt trouble on the road. However, presumably out of kindness, my mate took it upon himself to provide the base fire and with something approaching horror I observed large slabs of coal being propelled with brute force through the firehole. Quite rapidly a deep layer was laid on in this way and, with a friendly wink (a difficult business as he had a squint), he climbed off the engine, oilcan in hand, to apply a drop of lubricant in strategic places.

I took the opportunity to look into the firebox. A deep yellow fug was curling up between the cobbles, rapidly enveloping a cold brick arch. 'To the devil with this', I thought, opening up the damper and giving the jet a good turn. We duly backed up to our train and, after some initial trouble in coupling the vacuum and steam hose, I climbed into the cab. The steam-heater gauge was playing up—one minute around 30lb, the next streaking up to 80lb. This was noticed by my mate, who, somewhat shaken, scrambled over and adjusted it. It proved, however, to be one which I had frequently met—the non-adjustable type. No amount of coaxing would get it to remain at a set pressure. As events turned out, we shut it off completely later on, the steam thus saved being used to help us to keep going!

Rarely do I remember feeling quite so much on edge as on this return trip. My mate also was obviously nervous and anxious to get under way. For me, the fire was slow in responding; even the dart had little effect. The last few seconds seemed to creep by and every nerve in my body felt tense, waiting for something to happen. I pulled heavily on a cigarette and gripped the wheel of the injector steam-valve, peering up at the steam pressure-gauge located in the gloom near the roof of the cab. Pressure was slowly reaching the 200lb maximum mark, but, oh, so slowly! I eased the jet a bit and noted an almost immediate response on the gauge. Climbing a little faster now, I put the injector on to top up a little and dampen the dusty contents of the tender and the floor. A nervous sweat trickled down my cheeks and, coupled with the steamy cab atmosphere, made me more uncomfortable than ever. Would we never start?

These dreamlike thoughts were shattered by the whistle for 'right away', with an instant response from my mate. Slipping, sliding and banging, we got under way. I slammed the firehole door tight, leaned heavily against the cab side and extracted the last few puffs from the cigarette. We were thundering through Armley and intermittent showers of sparks and cinders were flying from the chimney top. I picked up the shovel to put a few shots up to the front of the box. A carefully prepared heap of broken coal had somehow disappeared under an avalanche of boulder-sized lumps. We just had to get more coal on. Wildly I struck at the lumps, while sharp splinters flew in showers around both my hands and my face. With great difficulty I managed to dislodge the main offender—a brute about three feet long and of similar width. Repeated blows with the coal pick had no effect and then the tender doors somehow jammed again. The showers of fire had increased to volcanic proportions now, with the rapidly vibrating firehole doors indicating a sizeable hole somewhere, while both steam pressure and water level were dropping.

By now we were climbing through Calverley to Thackley Tunnel. More steam was required and my mate had adjusted the reverser. He also had realised the situation, and in desperation we heaved enormous cobbles through the firehole door and with vicious kicks prayed that they would get to the desired spot in the box. Clouds of filthy smoke beat down on us and enveloped the cab, together with swirling steam pouring from somewhere at the front end. All the time the incessant banging, crashing, jarring and rolling continued.

As we approached Thackley Tunnel, we were losing speed badly, and twice when inside the tunnel the wheels slipped, despite the fact that the sanders had been applied. Time seemed to stand still as, with a steady thumping, banging and colossal roar, we threaded our way up the gradual incline. Thicker clouds of hot smoke and steam poured into the cab, making it difficult to breathe, and clouds of dust swirled round our heads and penetrated our inner clothing. Eventually the faint glow from the firehole gave way to a speck of light ahead, heralding the end of this journey through hell, the clouds of smoke and steam gave way to waves of night air. We had made it but at a terrible cost—barely an inch of water was now showing, and we had little more than 160lb of steam.

We slowed for the curve at Leeds Junction, Shipley, and once again I tried to break into the tender. Solid blocks of coal still jammed the entrance and even when the tender doors were opened the trouble still remained, for the net result of this action had been an avalanche, making shovelling in an already confined space quite impossible. Once again we had to resort to lumps. Continuous work with the coal pick had only a little result, partially owing to the very nature of the coal but mainly to the pick itself. This delightful tool had a metal head and shaft, and each blow transmitted such stinging shocks to one's hands that they positively ached with pain.

Keighley, our first stop, was reached about 6min late, with a 'dry' gauge glass, both injectors working, 160lb of steam and the jet hard on. Dripping with sweat, covered in dust and already very tired I managed to give the firebox a good pull through and raked some life into the cobbly firebed. We pulled out with water showing about one inch in the glass and in anything but a satisfactory order. One minute had been allowed at Keighley and we had lost a further two. There was a slight improvement over the nine miles or so to Skipton where we held our time loss at about the same level, but the water was still very low. Some smaller lumps of coal had appeared by now, and we left Skipton with clouds of smoke and cinders flying high into the sky, in an endeavour both to liven up the fire and also to pull back some lost time. The 4min allowance at Skipton was partly for taking water if necessary, but in our troubled state we had overshot the column here, and so had to bank on taking a supply at Hellifield instead.

The long bank through Gargrave and Bell Busk gradually took its toll and despite desperate efforts we lost further time. By now the fire was in somewhat better shape, but working heavily in an attempt to gain lost time and with my added difficulty in firing from the right-hand side, the pressure had gradually fallen back. To add to our troubles the injector on my side became stubborn and started to blow back. Shutting this off, and putting on the other injector, on the driver's side, we lost a valuable part of our boiler reserve. All these trials and tribulations could not dampen the feeling of pleasure, however, as over the summit we cantered down into Hellifield—late, it is true, but still on the move, all the same!

Probably because the steam pressure was somewhat reduced and coupled with our anxiety not to lose much more time—we stopped with the tank filler opposite the column, instead of a little ahead of it. With all speed the leather delivery pipe was handed on to the tender top and thrust into the hole, and my mate turned the water full on. I am not sure what actually happened next, but with considerable violence the 'bag', as we called it, burst out of the tender, landed over my shoulder and soaked me to the skin. There was no time for sympathy; in went the 'bag' again and this time it stayed in.

Hellifield station is in a very isolated position; it is always cold and windy and this particular night was no exception. Rapidly I froze and shivered, my teeth started to chatter and a miserable feeling swept over me. After all we had been through, this soaking had had to happen. The tank filled, I leapt quickly back into the cab and thrust a quick round of coal into the box. Steam and water were now much better and I could take stock of the situation. My shirt and vest were wet through, my overalls were not much better, and my shoes were full of water. My mate insisted on leaving the firehole door open in order to keep me warm. So I stripped off my shirt and vest and laid them on suitably hot pipes to dry out and then slipped back into my overall jacket. Fortunately I had discarded this earlier, to allow myself more movement to attack the jammed tender. This incident had a dual effect on us—it cheered my mate up no end and freshened me considerably.

The net result was a great endeavour to regain time. We took full advantage of the favourable down-grade towards Settle and the Junction was taken at a headlong sprint. The crashing and the banging seemed to evaporate as harder and harder we worked her to attack the short but sharp bank past Giggleswick. I do not think I have ever climbed this stretch of 1 in 100 faster. We tore over the top and down through Eldroth and on to Clapham like a thunderbolt. Our engine was the thunder, and a solid stream of fire thrown over the surrounding moors represented lightning—at least it seemed so to me that night!

To suggest that the curve through Clapham Junction was taken on four wheels instead of eight would be an obvious exaggeration, but I do not know how we held the track. My mate had two objectives now. The first was to reach Heysham on time, and the second to get me back to the shed to dry off properly. Steam was kept on all the way downhill to Bentham, after which we braked at Wennington for the junction, and then opened out fully once again. I have never had such a wild but exciting ride; lineside cottages and bridges seemed to streak by and in no time we had to shut off steam at the power-station on the approach to Lancaster. There is little more to add. With the help of a recovery time in our schedule, we did succeed in reaching Heysham dead on time, after a night of what seemed to me hell and glory in equal measure, but thankfully with a happy ending. Incidentally, my vest and shirt had both dried out, and much of the travel-stained image up to Hellifield had been removed by my impromptu bath. Numerous cuts, burns and bruises had been collected, however, and remained for quite some time as a reminder of that epic run. I felt very proud that night for although very tired, I had overcome all troubles and had helped to bring the boat train into Heysham on time.

Lest I have given the impression that all the locomotives with which we had to deal were predominantly in bad order, let me now hasten to correct this. Among the motley selection of machines at Lancaster were a number of Fowler 'Crab' 2–6–0s, Nos 42893/95 and 42928. Here at last I met engines that to me were constant friends. They were not particularly handsome, perhaps, nor very smooth riders, but they could be relied on to do two things—to steam and to pull. No run was ever a struggle with one of these engines, and even with a heavy load a good hard pull could be guaranteed.

For free steaming the only equals of the 'Crabs' were the 3F 0–6–0s. No art was required in firing the 'Crabs', just a steady six to ten shots, fairly evenly round the grate, and they would take both injectors—full on, if necessary. They were really enormously powerful machines and rarely lost their feet. Surprisingly a test report of the maximum boiler output of these engines, did not compare favourably with more modern locomotives of the same power classification. If only their riding had been a little less left-right, they would have licked Class 5 4–6–0 on any duty. 'Stronger' injectors would have been an improvement, but one cannot have everything and to me they were a near-ideal locomotive, giving a wonderful performance without requiring too much skill and persuasion on the part of the crew. During my footplate days I had them on several express passenger runs, going all out, safety-valve sizzling, both injectors on, but the boiler steadily emptying! For a while the 'Crabs' were rated 6P5F—who the optimist was I do not know, but they were certainly '5-*plus*' engines.

I once met a Newton Heath driver who spent over an hour extolling their virtues to me, finally stating that they'd lift a train up the side of Blackpool Tower if given the chance. A rather different type of compliment was applied to some other engines—2Ps in particular—was that they would slip even on Blackpool sands!

It is curious that many of the modern small and medium-powered locomotives seemed inferior to their older counterparts. One could, of course, only compare engines that were similar in power or that directly replaced older types, but this is not always a just comparison. However, one is hardly likely to impress an engine-crew with a machine, no matter how new and loaded with gadgets, that does not show up as well as the machine that has been displaced.

For example, neither of the two Ivatt designs of 2–6–0 were outstanding. The small 464XX 2–6–0s, despite their cab comforts and rocking grates, fell well short of the Midland or LYR Class 2F 0–6–0s in many other respects. Their ability to steam showed a limitation which was not apparent with the older engines. Further, they took longer to raise steam, a task which had to be accomplished with a fairly liberal use of the jet. The larger 430XX 2–6–0s were even less of a gift, and when one removed the 'frills' one found them less responsive than a good 4F 0–6–0. The steep inclination of the grate produced the same firing difficulties as with a 4F, and oscillation quickly worked the fire deep under the arch. In their original double-chimney condition they were ravenous beasties with two 'insides', half the fuel landing on top of the arch to provide a second fire, or vanishing through the tubes and out of the chimney.

The injectors, which admittedly were very powerful, needed to be, for as well as being very hungry these engines were also very thirsty. The pull-out regulators may have had some mystic hidden improvement that I never discovered, but in practice they were extremely stubborn to open and close; we thought that this regulator may have been two-handled in order to allow both men to operate it! The accessible motion soon became very filthy, and the absence of splashers allowed deposits of filth and dust to penetrate every crack and crevice of the locomotive (and crew!); hence, no doubt, the claim of 'accessibility'. The one small consolation was the whistle, which indeed was most powerful and melodious, a delightful sound to relieve an aggravated soul after a troublesome trip and something to distract one from the major issues. It is only fair to add that these engines with single blastpipes were somewhat better machines than those with double chimneys, though hardly a notable advance in steam power.

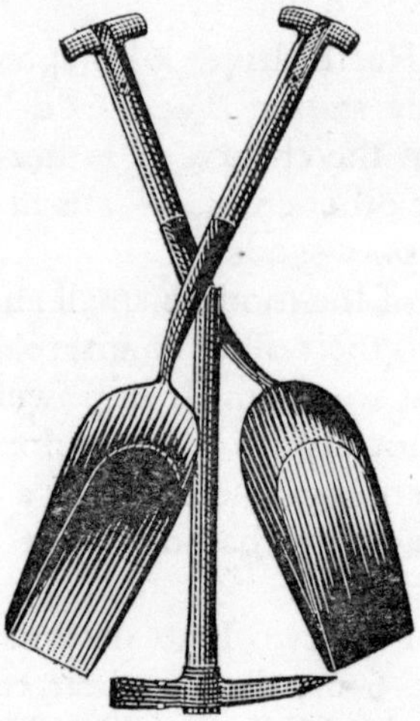

4

Engine Preparation and Disposal

When writing about life on the footplate and the idiosyncrasies of various engines, one tends to overlook the fact that at some depots both drivers and firemen had to work very hard on the principal shed duties, which were the preparation and disposal of locomotives. On the LMS the Midland Division sheds had proper disposal links, with engine-crews cleaning the fires, smokeboxes and ashpans. The LNW Division, however, generally employed labourers for this unpleasant task, thus respecting the status of enginemen. There can be no doubt that fire-cleaning and dropping was *the* most unpleasant duty a shed could provide; it was sheer, exacting hell. Not only were fires often solid blocks of clinker up to a foot thick, but so many engines—eight, if I remember correctly—constituted a day's work, and sometimes the driver, if he was that kind of person, had but two aims—to stand around and watch the sweat pouring off his mate and to keep his eyes on the clock.

Subject to there being sufficient engines to dispose of, one could perhaps do one's quota in four to five hours. Now this meant real hard labour, with different engines requiring different techniques for clinker extraction, some with small or cluttered cabs being real villains to clean. The fireman, as fire-cleaner, had two methods. One was to clean the firebox by pushing the good top fire to the middle of the grate and removing all the clinker in the back half, dragging all the clinker from the front over the mound of good fire, shovelling this out, and finally pulling the clean fire under the fire-hole. Alternatively, he could clear a section of the grate, remove two or three firebars, and gradually move all the dross and clinker through the gap. No doubt the reader would choose the latter way as appearing to be far the simpler, and on paper so would I.

But wait—there is a little snag. To remove these long and heavy iron firebars a wonderful man-sized pair of tongs was provided. These tongs gave only a partial grip, and successful removal of a firebar depended on a good flick of the wrist. This movement could have one of two results; the bar either slipped through the firehole as intended or fell into the ashpan. Unfortunately, when I cleaned fires by this method, the bars usually did the latter. Here they sometimes became wedged and, in any case, proved difficult to remove intact, for the ashpan rake would deposit them on the brick floor of the pit, often in two pieces. Even if intact, they were too hot to handle and had to be left to cool. Now it always paid to keep the steam-raisers sweet and even-tempered, and nothing was more calculated to enrage these gentlemen than to have engines stowed away on shed without their full complement of firebars.

All this being clearly understood, I usually opted for the more arduous 'baling out' method. In any event, as some mates would not clean out the ashpan bar removal was taboo, for to succeed with this method required two active persons—one pushing the clinker through the top and the other pulling it out of the bottom. I know no other method of losing surplus weight so quickly as fire-cleaning. I did several months' regular fire-dropping, at both Lancaster and Burton, and lost several stone in the course of these duties.

The ashpit showed the true competence of one's fellow fireman or the appalling state of the fuel—whichever way you chose to look at it. Not infrequently an engine would arrive on the ashpit and the crew would be seen hurrying off to the time-office almost before it had stopped. Now this was usually a bad sign. It often meant that, somehow or other, the brick arch and the fire had become one, or, to put it another way, the box was bung full. At the very least, this would require an hour of chopping, digging and slicing to excavate to the bars, presuming that arch had not expired on top of the mound. If this happened then one not only had to excavate, but nearly to expire at the same time, and this is not to be confused with perspiration, which in any event was unlimited.

Removing a fallen arch was rather like baling out lumps of lead and one's arms rapidly became numbed and mechanical. The sheer weight and thickness of these 'volcanic tips' bent and softened as many as two or three paddles and as many darts. The acid-laden fumes rising from the pit beneath and from the engine during fire-cleaning filled one's mouth with a bitter taste, dried the back of the throat and made the eyes sore. Hands became hard, burned, horny objects; overalls, soaked daily in sweat, rotted and fell apart; while the life of a pair of boots was halved through clambering about on piles of hot clinker. Apart from a good fire, the contents of a firebox were not always clinker and lumps of brick-arch; one often struck an immovable mass which, more often than not, was the remains of

Opposite: *Tables showing Rate of Firing selected LMR Locomotives. Extract from Report, prepared by the Dept. of Operational Research, British Railways Board.* See *Chap. 12, p. 126.* (B. Rail)

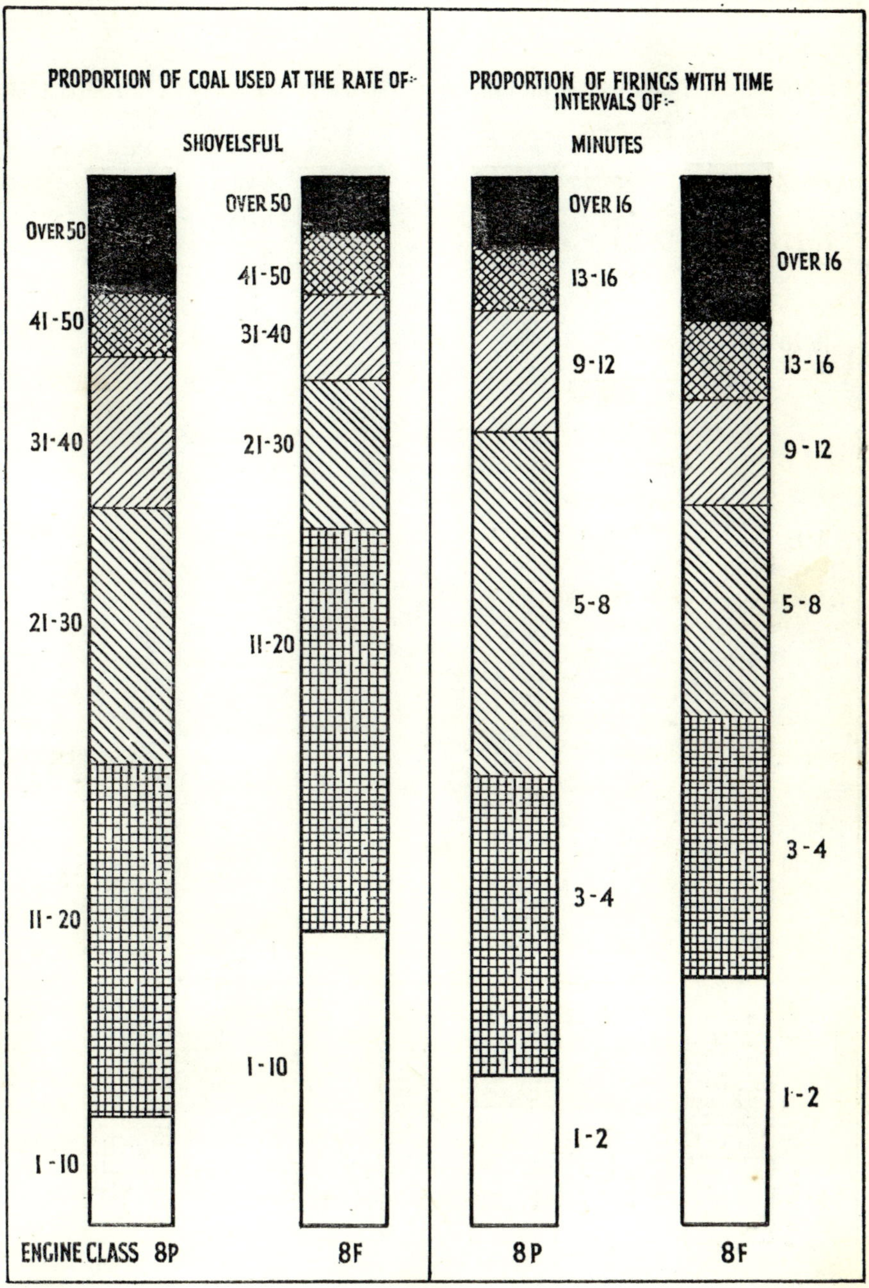
PROPORTION OF COAL USED AT THE RATE OF:-
SHOVELSFUL
OVER 50
41-50
31-40
21-30
11-20
1-10
OVER 50
41-50
31-40
21-30
11-20
1-10
ENGINE CLASS 8P
8F
PROPORTION OF FIRINGS WITH TIME INTERVALS OF:-
MINUTES
OVER 16
13-16
9-12
5-8
3-4
1-2
OVER 16
13-16
9-12
5-8
3-4
1-2
8P
8F

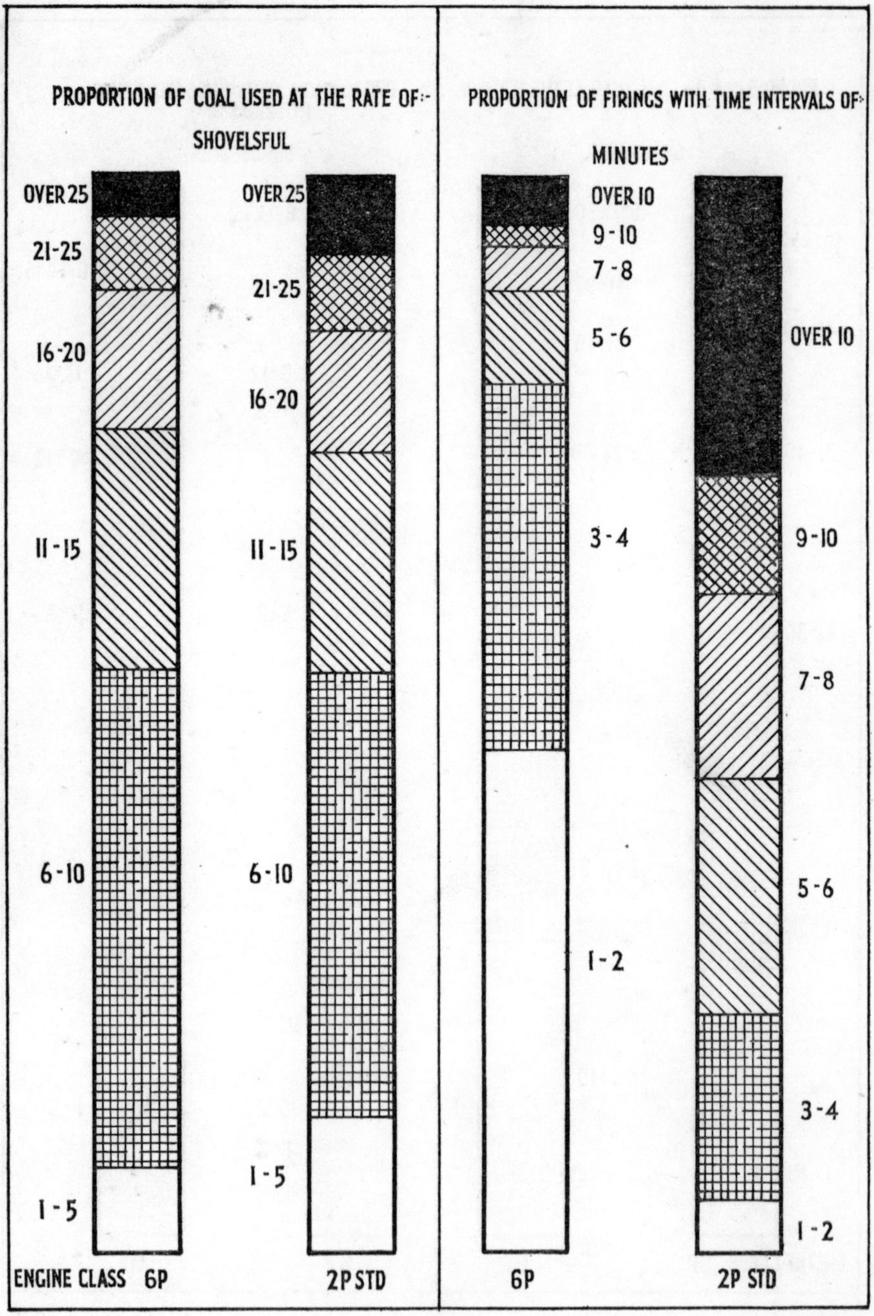
PROPORTION OF COAL USED AT THE RATE OF:-
SHOVELSFUL
OVER 25
21-25
16-20
11-15
6-10
1-5
OVER 25
21-25
16-20
11-15
6-10
1-5
PROPORTION OF FIRINGS WITH TIME INTERVALS OF:-
MINUTES
OVER 10
9-10
7-8
5-6
3-4
1-2
OVER 10
9-10
7-8
5-6
3-4
1-2
ENGINE CLASS 6P
2P STD
6P
2P STD

the baffle-plate. This, having fallen into the fire, had fused to the bars, which often meant the loss of several bars as well.

Engines which had been running with full ashpans often presented a whole set of badly-burned bars, and I once saw this happen on a Class 5 4-6-0, with rocker-bars, at Crewe. The whole grate had been so badly burned that, with very little aid, the entire grate collapsed and fell through the hopper into the pit—a complete write-off.

Many engines arrived on the ashpits not only with thick dead fires, but with about 70lb of steam and very little water in the boiler. These conditions provided two problems; quick cleaning and coaling and often a struggle to get the engine on to the shed. Once on the shed, whatever the steam pressure, it was the steam-raiser's problem. Very bad cases, when put away on their respective shed roads, required the boiler to be topped up by means of a pump to ensure a sufficient safety margin. Smokeboxes were often worse than fireboxes, full of ash to the top of the blast-pipe. An unwary soul would swing the door open to find himself buried up to the ankles in an avalanche of ash. Some types were cleaned only once a week or so, and a careful note was kept of when this task was last done.

After the fire had been attended to and the tender filled, the next operation was coaling. This was done by means of an electric crane, hoisting tubs which were tipped into the tender while suspended above it. In most cases this was just routine, but some engines required a really good supply and this meant careful stacking in order to get the maximum quantity on. Large lumps were stood up along the sides to hold a centre peak, and to prevent this from rolling off and causing injury or damage.

Preparation, the other main shed job at Lancaster, was quite a simple matter, for the driver usually oiled up the engine and all the fireman had to do was to ensure that it had a full complement of tools, to fill the lamps and sanders (if required), to clean up the cab and to make good the fire and boiler. All this was rather too good to be true, of course, and the usual problem was finding the tools. Lancaster had a permanent shortage of engine tackle. To keep the show going one robbed each incoming engine to supply the next outgoing one. With luck this system would suffice. However, when the supply of incoming engines ran out and one still had several engines to prepare, trouble ensued. To add to this state of crisis, several sets of men might be preparing at the same time, and a fireman would not bat an eyelid when carefully removing tools from an engine already prepared by someone else to make up the quota on his own, which might be due off shed first.

To highlight this situation, I will use as an example one of the Heysham shunts, due off shed about 8pm to work a trip from New Zealand Yard to Heysham and relieve one of the other engines. This engine might be out for 18 or 24 hours, and consequently required a good bunker of coal. When on this duty one prepared the engine, filled the firebox, particularly at the back end, left a heap of coal in the cab, and then dropped by the coal stage to ensure the fullest possible supply. One tried to have about 10 to 15min before leaving the shed to brew tea and have a sandwich. One day we had completed all these duties as usual, had spent our ten minutes having a cup of tea and then left the shed and hooked up to our train. I had opened the damper and hotted her up and decided to pop a few shots under the arch to get her really going, suddenly to discover that I had no shovel! Some so-and-so had removed it during the ten minutes we had spent in the mess-room. A more serious case occurred at Crewe when someone stole my engine's headlamps and we had but a minute before the 'right away'. These manœuvres were all caused by shortage. Most depots kept a careful check on tools; one signed for them and returned them to the tool stores at the end of a trip. At Lancaster the tools were supposed to stop on the engines all the time. Pilfering and loss, coupled with difficulty in obtaining replacements in sufficient quantity, caused the shortage.

Most of the shed duties were covered by men who had been removed from the main line or who, for various reasons, were confined to the shed. Of these undoubtedly the greatest character at Lancaster shed was an old LYR man of mammoth proportions and a very peculiar state of mind. No one quite knew his exact history. He had apparently been attached to many depots in the course of his career, and had had more than his share of accidents and troubles. His record, indeed, was studded with a list of derailments, collisions and flattened buffer-stops, culminating in his finally being confined to the ashpit. He had no friends and, being slightly deaf, he spoke in a series of sharp grunts. Among his many vices was a shocking temper, more akin to fits of rage. He was easy prey to provocation and reacted with surprising violence. His main weapons were on his feet—a pair of enormous unlaced clogs. Had you been fool enough to enrage him and, further, to remain in his presence, he was more than liable to lift a leg with surprising speed, propelling a clog with tremendous force and at the same time giving vent to a fount of oaths and curses. In his most dangerous mood he could throw fire-irons like javelins, and woe betide the slow mover!

He was often quoted as the main character in the 'Electric Train Tale'. The story goes that one day, during a run on the old electric trains from Morecambe to Heysham, a lady happened to enquire of the railwayman beside her as to who the driver was that day. The man replied that he himself was, thus giving her an awful fright. Apparently he occasionally left the driver's cab and walked through the train, passing the time of day with the passengers. Presumably any 'deadman's handle' was securely tied down. Even as part of the shed staff he could be involved in trouble, and he had been responsible for knocking down several stop-blocks. On one occasion I believe his engine passed through the stop-block and the shed fenced enclosure, and landed up in the road leading to the station. Much of this trouble could be attributed to his own heavy-handedness and to the policy of the steam-raisers, who persistently filled boilers 'up to the whistle'. But this bad-tempered shed man met his match one day with a D class 0–8–0. He sailed past the shed, making for a raft of wagons down by the warehouse. As he passed one could see that all the colour had drained from his face, on which there was a look of terror. Eventually he hit the wagons with some force but, fortunately, without serious damage.

'Super-Ds' (LNW 0–8–0s) and compounds with overfilled boilers were particularly prone to becoming 'hydraulic' as soon as the regulator was opened and to stop an engine in this state with, perhaps, 40 to 50lb of steam on the clock, was almost an impossibility. I remember being caught with a compound in this state, coming off the shed on to the turntable. It wasn't going to stop, so I reversed and stopped with the aid of the engine in the rear! Looking back now, I realise how lucky I was to have had something to fall back on!

A glance at the diagram of Green Ayre shed will provide the reader with the location of Cable Street siding or spur, so named after the parallel main road. Often when the shed and adjoining roads were becoming uncomfortably full one was told to put such-and-such an engine 'down Cable Street'; for my part this kindled an earnest desire to do so literally, just to see the ensuing reactions.

Characters like the erratic shed-man just mentioned and the driver of No 43890 were very much the exception. I had some good and understanding mates. There was 'Bob', a short, beaming-faced ex-'Lanky' driver, who had come to Lancaster with several others when Colne shed closed in 1932. He was an absolute stickler for a clean cab, proper firing and doing what you were told. Gradually I mastered matters, and thanks to his understanding, I settled down with him. Routine and reason were substituted for the uncertainty of hit and miss. He was a fine example of engineman. Always clean, neat and tidy in himself, he expected just the same of his mate. He taught me how and when to oil or clean and to make up a fire; later on, how to shunt. During a lengthy spell at Heysham, I brought the latter to a very fine art. One proud night I broke up a raft of 20-odd wagons into five lots, and then had them all rolling to different points and still moving, with the engine smartly drawn up at the water-column, and myself observant and waiting for the first batch to reach its destination. 'Fly shunting', and a host of other tricks, such as rapid reverse, were things I gloried in. In later days I had a lot to thank Bob for; my early resentment had blossomed into admiration. He was a good driver and loved the old LYR.

Big Bill (ex-LYR also) was another able driver I shall never forget. He would not tolerate swearing at any price, and he hated 'Teddy' firemen. By then the generation of 'Teddy boys' had reached the footplate, and he took a personal delight in making them conform precisely to the rules. Another driver, the 'Hymn-singer', was a menace. From start to finish it was psalms, hymns and religion generally. He never mentioned anything else. Perhaps the best driver I ever had was J. B. Moore. 'J.B.' was a character. Of medium height and with sallow features, beady eyes and a hook nose, he wore, in addition to his ordinary uniform, clogs and an old suit jacket, and had the cheek of the devil. Originally from Wigan, I believe, he appeared to have worked over most of north-west England in his time. Again of LYR background, what he didn't know about an engine I shouldn't think mattered. He was a near genius; he could fire and drive a fully-laden engine anywhere, with no slipping and no smoke—driving to perfection. Economy and care should have been his motto. Like many 'Lanky' men he had been trained in engine matters at the Manchester School of Technology, and had a superb knowledge of the locomotive.

He was the only driver I ever had who could adjust the brake properly, deal competently with a 'sticky' injector, correctly tighten a leaky valve-packing and cure a stiff regulator. The latter trick was accomplished by inserting a few drops of engine oil into the gauge-glass through the top nut which, incidentally, did not cause priming. This, coupled with a waste pad soaked in engine oil put on the regulator spindle, always worked. Knocks and blows were automatically located, sticking cylinder taps were freed, and sanders produced sand!

A veritable 'Merlin', he exerted a curious influence over me; he made me think about every move before I made it. Nothing should be done unnecessarily, he always used to imply. Even with his back to me I knew he was aware of what I was going to do next—still more, what I *should* do next. Regulator, reverser, brake, all became alive and full of meaning and were handled with a precision I have never met with in anyone else. 'J.B.' was a crack engineman. Often his temper was tried, especially by shunters and signalmen. If there was a means of retaliation, he used it. Anyone who upset him really went through it. A torrent of broad 'Lancashire' was evoked, and the recipient was glad to retreat!

Firing became a wonderful art. With him I have seen, as his fireman, the near-impossible performed. A firebox with the bars showing could produce more steam than we could ever use, with no smoke and hardly any clinker. Dampers were instruments of precision and not just levers that opened and closed. Every trip with him was an education in itself. He bragged, oh, how he bragged, but I am certain that it was always with full justification.

Top Link compound handlers always had a moan—either the engines were too rough, or had no steam, or a dozen and one other complaints. But 'J.B.' would growl and snort and, with a contemptuous spit, would declare himself able, single-handed, to get to Leeds with ten minutes in hand, and burn at least a tub less coal as well, all with four more coaches on! Oddly enough, I am sure he could have done it.

The other side of 'J.B.' was equally devastating. He had an amazing repertoire of bar-room ditties, songs and verse. A constant stream of old Lancashire 'pub' songs and rhymes were provided as entertainment on every trip, together with occasional accompaniment in the form of a clog dance. With an expressionless face he would accomplish turn after turn of ventriloquism, mime, whistling, all with equal ability. Every trip was a lesson, not merely in enginemanship but in human competence, with this cool wonderful mate. Of all the drivers for whom I ever fired 'J.B.' would be my choice, anywhere, on any engine—we should always have got there, and as quickly and efficiently as possible. Taken as a whole, ex-LYR drivers were more able and knowledgeable than any others I ever worked with. Engines seemed second nature to them, and nothing about them was a mystery. They had confidence and a pure love of the job. Everything should and could work. Engines were to be mastered at all times; never, never must they master the crew—neither fireman nor driver.

Hours and hours of engine chat about one type or another took place on the shunts and I began to know the ins-and-outs of most LYR and Crewe engines, and many others too. At times enthusiasm reached a *crescendo* and vicious attacks on the Midland took place—on their engines, their men and their policy. Several drivers wore the LYR button in their hats, just to show that the wretched 'Wyvern' was not the only survival of the glorious days of the individual companies.

I well remember a less competent driver, too. He was of a nervous type and was a rather pathetic soul, who at some time in his career had committed an unforgivable blunder. It appears that during one trip his engine ran out of water up on the hills and far from the nearest water-column. In sheer terror he managed to contact the local fire-brigade, which eventually appeared, presumably over the moors, and pumped him safe again. Being of a naturally nervous disposition, he was quite a trial to be with. He consumed at least thirty Woodbines on every trip, while constant worry and nagging upset every turn of duty. Sanders were rodded and prodded at every stop, and the oil-can feeder almost smoked with the frequency of its use. Terror appeared in his poor old eyes when the water got an inch down the gauge glass; the pressure gauge was under constant surveillance and five pounds from the red line was a crisis; signals were things to be hunted miles away, with feverish leaps and crouchings in curious positions to try and get a previously unheard-of view of their message. Never have I seen a man in such a dither. Beads of sweat would appear on his brow while the brake took hold and heaved itself into action. Phantom howls from signal-boxes and imaginary explosions from detonators would be heard, the tender water gauge was continually consulted and the injector checked for any possible leakage. Poor chap! My last sight of him was crouched by a 4F, wire in hand, prodding a reluctant sand pipe, while his fireman looked on with complete understanding and, I suspect, not a little sympathy.

One of the shed's more colourful drivers, a man of rather Romany appearance, suffered from intermittent bouts of the 'devil'. By this I mean that he was temperamental, to say the least. This condition was said to have been brought about by an unfortunate contact with overhead electric wires while he was in the act of using a fire-iron. He was probably one of the few cases who lived to tell the tale. His wild changes of temperament caused firemen to dread having to work with him for long periods. Sometimes meek and quite casual in his handling of a locomotive, he would suddenly become demented and flog his engine unmercifully, causing his fireman much extra labour. During such periods of hell-bent passion, his engine could be heard when still very far from the shed.

The outcast exists everywhere, even on engines, and our outcast was a short, stocky soul with greasy brown features, filthy overalls and jacket, and a pair of dirty cracked hands, gnarled and sometimes gnawed if he was hungry enough. To all appearances he was the typical down-and-out. Rather sheepish, furtive-looking, slightly distrustful, and with instinct more animal than human, T. . . . and I became acquainted on my first lodging trip and consequently I recollect events quite clearly. I was very excited and announced with great pride at home my trip on the 'lodger' for the next day. Special care was taken in getting clean overalls, shining shoes and a decent shirt, together with ample supplies of food wrapped in a beautiful white linen serviette and deposited in a good-sized sandwich box. The brass buckle on my belt and the Furness Railway button in my hat (an acquired mascot) were both given an extra special shine. After all, it was one of our best jobs, so I had better look good, even if my performance was not. I decided to go to the shed with plenty of time in hand to give the fire a good build-up, and to get the cab into reasonably clean order.

When booking on, the time-clerk gave me engine No. 43034 and told me who was to be my mate, though the latter point did not mean very much to me, as I had not previously been with him. The engine at that time had a double chimney and with a short and somewhat steeply-inclined grate did not offer the best of prospects. Quite a lot of difficulty had been met in keeping time with this type of engine owing to poor steaming. After about an hour spent in general preparation and feeling satisfied that I had done all I reasonably could, I went to the mess to brew a can of tea, all set for the journey. I came back to find that my mate had arrived and was settling himself in. The contrast between us was rather startling. On the one hand my spotless overalls, clean shirt, and shining boots and brass—and on the other a scruffy, dirty, untidy little man, who could not have washed for some considerable time past. A very greasy haversack was deposited in the clothes cupboard and we were ready to start.

Things turned out very much as I expected. By Bentham we were having quite a struggle and a large quantity of small coal had landed on top of the arch while the remainder had worked too quickly up to the front end. With frequent use of the rocker and of the coal rake we managed to top Clapham and had some respite going down to Hellifield. During this time T. . . . had been very understanding and had eased the engine considerably, telling me not to worry; we had enough steam, he said, and was generally encouraging, even to the extent of doing a little firing himself (though not so well as I had done, I thought). At last we arrived in Leeds and made for our lodge, which turned out to be a depressingly grimy building about fifty yards from the coal-stage at Holbeck shed. T. . . . took pains to ensure that I knew the ropes and showed a somewhat fatherly approach.

After a good wash I adjourned to the mess-room to have my meal. I selected a table, unfolded my sandwiches and proceeded to eat. While I had been getting my food ready and making a cup of tea, T. . . . had been having a large white basin warmed up and, selecting some choice wedges of bread, he came and sat down beside me. There were several other sets of men and I had been chatting to another fireman, when gradually I noticed a somewhat embarrassing silence, broken by deep sucking and gurgling noises. My mate was devouring his stew-like supper without cutlery of any sort and apparently without even bothering to wash. That he was enjoying it was quite obvious, for he made no pause, despite trails of brown fatty liquid trickling down under his chin.

There was a silence born of shock as, one by one, heads had turned to see the rather pitiful spectacle, somewhat reminiscent of the workhouse. I proceeded to dispose of my supper as quickly as possible and to make myself scarce. Finally I decided to have a pint or two and went off to a floodlit football match at the Elland Road ground. Arriving back at the barracks, I found our bedroom containing three beds, chose one and climbed into it. T. . . . appeared very shortly afterwards, armed with three chamber-pots, one each of which he tossed to myself and the guard, who had the third bed. Stripping down to his long underwear and belching a few times, he sang a little ditty, wished us goodnight, and fell asleep.

This trip had an interesting sequel, however. We sampled Holbeck's pride and joy—an electric turntable. This wonderful machine was equipped with a smart control panel, little lights and a host of button gadgets. Amongst these was what was called an 'inching button'. With ordinary vacuum-operated tables, a certain amount of calculating was required to ensure that the brake-pin dropped into the correct hole. Often the table received severe jolting by having this brake-pin locked in whilst it was moving round too fast. The result was a stop which did little to prolong the life of the turntable, the whole thing, complete with engine, coming to a particularly abrupt and shattering halt. With the electric table at Holbeck, however, one used the motor to all but the last foot or so, when the 'inching button' moved the last short distance to the selected brake-hole with absolutely no shock or shuddering. For some time, until the novelty either wore off or staff became short, the table had an attendant who instructed and assisted with the turning.

Reverting to other matters, derailments on Green Ayre shed were quite frequent, though usually of a quite trivial character. A more serious one in which I was involved took place one foggy day just before the usual morning exodus of engines. I had been detailed to hold a pair of facing points to stow three engines out of the way prior to their leaving for their duties. As to what actually happened I have never been quite sure, but someone called them back before I had got the points hard over. The result was one-and-a-half engines off the rails. If I remember correctly, I was off duty at 7am and all the following day, expecting at any moment to be suspended from duty. Fortunately, however, I heard nothing more. On another occasion, when I was in charge of No 41903, her rear end dropped over the turntable perimeter and took quite a lot of righting.

The odd shed collision caused much bad feeling and fists would sometimes be swung by the shocked and frightened parties involved. Most accidents at the shed were not, however, the cause of carelessness so much as due to the general congestion caused by the peculiar layout of the shed and its servicing facilities. Most sheds seemed to suffer from periods of congestion and sometimes the resulting tangles took some sorting out, by a diplomat of the first order, to preserve order and tempers.

Towards the end of my career at Lancaster my family moved to Kirby Lonsdale, 16 miles away. Hours and lack of money decreed that I should cycle to and from work, and the 32 miles of exercise through all weathers, *plus* my work, became something of an ordeal. I lost a lot of weight and my days became a long succession of work and sleep. It was during this time that the ASLEF decided to call a strike right in the middle of summer.

BR standard Class 2 2–6–0 No 78016 on the Whithorn branch goods at Millisle, Gallway in May 1964 *Derek Cross*

Ivatt Class 2 2-6-0 No 46400 passing Carnforth M.P.D. with a ballast train in June 1966 *B. J. Ashworth*

Class 2F 0-6-0 No 58246, the last engine of this class to retain a round-top firebox *T. C. Lawrence*

An LNWR 0–8–0 approaching Bedford Station with a train of ballast hoppers in 1959 *M. S. Welch*

Broadside view of ex-LNW 0–8–0 No 49180 *E. R. Wetherself*

Fowler 0–8–0 No 49618 passing Gledholt Box on a Diggle Healey Mills empties *Kenneth Field*

'Crab' 2-6-0 No 42925 restarting a northbound freight after a stop immediately north of Tebay for a banker in June 1961 *Derek Cross*

The Lakeside branch terminus in July 1965 with a Lakeside–Ulverston train headed by Class 5 4-6-0 No 45025 *Derek Cross*

The 12 noon Lakeside–Ulverston local passing Newby Bridge old halt, a Class 5 4–6–0 in charge *W. H. Foster*

Preparing for the road at Speke Junction m.p.d. on May 26, 1966 is Stanier Class 5 4–6–0 No 45071 *Ian G. Holt*

Class 5 4–6–0 No 45025 nears Clifton & Lowther with an excursion from Carlisle to Morecambe in August 1960 *J. E. Wilkinson*

A Class 5 4–6–0 entering Linslade Tunnel

Class 8F 2-8-0 No 48158 passing the closed station of Bell Busk with an up Settle-Carlisle line goods

Derek Cross

Beattock Bank, near Greskine, in July 1964: BR Standard Class 5 4-6-0 No 73098 on a Blackpool-Glasgow relief

Derek Cross

My position as regards the Union had always been rather peculiar. I joined, as did most youngsters, because one hadn't a sufficiently good reason for not doing so. However, although I soon recognised the necessity for joining and approved their actions, I always felt that we were barking up the wrong tree and should fight as hard to improve our working conditions and the locomotives as we appeared to fight for wages. Over the years I let my subscription slide, and while technically still a member, I felt rather an outsider. The imminent approach of the strike rather put me on a spot. I had no particular wish to leave my work, but any thought of independent action quickly vanished when I saw the attitude of the more militant fraternity. Frankly I hadn't the guts to go to work, so I took a sort of enforced holiday. Pickets were arranged, and I actually took part in one, but when the Union officials realised how far I had travelled to picket, they promptly excused me and told me to stop at home for the duration of the strike.

The return to work was with a certain sense of reluctance. I had had the most wonderful holiday of my life, with superb cloudless days. Back at work there was a decidedly unpleasant atmosphere and I was buttonholed several times by larger and older persons and warned not in any circumstances to talk to any NUR drivers I might be booked to work with.

Some of the staff flatly refused to work with NUR men, and gradually I formed a picture of what had happened during the strike. It appeared that the NUR, which was not involved in the strike, had an agreement whereby its members would only work their booked regular duties. In actual fact, at many depots, Lancaster included, certain non-striking crews worked anything and everything, with hours and hours of overtime. Crews from as far away as Royston and Normanton had worked our tank trains (oil and chemical) and coal trains, putting in something like 16 hours a day. Naturally enough, the ASLEF crews took a very dim view of this and the hard core were particularly angry. Indeed, physical violence was used at some places on men who had broken the agreement, and at the end of the strike the worst offenders never returned to the footplate, but received positions in the offices, as deputy foremen or some equivalent occupation.

Crewe had such an example. One man, who was reputed to have achieved many thousands of miles of work during the strike, was not allowed back on the footplate but received a very pleasant job, allocating engines to trains and controlling their position on the shed. What perhaps was worse was that the strike achieved so little and the younger members in particular lost considerable faith in the Union. Even to this date the situation has changed but little, and the 'blacklegs' are still not forgotten, for enginemen have long memories.

By now my days at Lancaster were drawing to a close. I had been bitten with the *wanderlust*, and decided to try for a change of scenery. I should leave behind me memories of some wonderful times, good trips and good mates, and I should take with me a fund of experience to apply to my future footplate work. What I did not realise at the time was that much of this experience would not be called on again until I got to Crewe.

In many ways I was sad to leave Lancaster. I loved the line over the hills to Skipton and the pretty stretches of river, the gradual change in scenery from the flat country around Morecambe and Heysham, up the Lune Valley, and the mile upon mile of rugged open moorland. The great flat top of Ingleborough overshadowed these moors, sometimes bright with heather and mosses, and yet bleak and lonely in wintertime, grey and cold or deep in snow which drifted high over the small stone walls that partitioned the lower moorland down into Craven and farther towards Leeds. The countryside in the north-west of England was home to me and I loved all of it, whatever part I was in. The area around Morecambe Bay towards Grange and Ulverston was beautiful in a different way, relying on the sea and the flat sands to provide contrast.

All this I was leaving behind, together with all the engines I had come to regard almost as my own, for at Lancaster one worked mainly on one's own engines rather than on foreign ones, and consequently knew them inside out, with all their little faults and peculiarities. Neither scenically nor in many other ways was I destined to find the same attractions at Burton-on-Trent, to which I was now to transfer myself.

5

Interlude at Burton-on-Trent

After the variety of work and engines at Lancaster, Burton was something of an anti-climax. Much of the work was of a shunting or trip nature about the various yards. There was very little main-line work, and this was entrusted to the older hands; never once did I get anything more inspiring than a ballast job on the main line, or a run to Uttoxeter. Just prior to my arrival the regular 'control relief' of coal trains north and south of Burton had practically ceased and consequently young hands were virtually confined to one or other of the main shunting duties. Frankly, I had not bargained for constant shunting and trip work, but the next few months were to provide no change.

Shunting has its interesting side and quite a lot of useful experience can be derived from it, but after a time it becomes simply monotonous, and it will never teach one to fire and handle big engines. There is simply no comparison. A completely different approach to firing methods is required on big engines. A box of fire on a shunt will last the best part of an hour or longer; provided that one keeps the pressure constant and smoke and blowing-off to a minimum one has nothing to fear, and the longer one is on this type of duty the less competent one is likely to be on a big engine. On shunting duties one is more like an attendant—a necessary task but not supremely so. The only release from monotony is on the driving side. Here one is constantly receiving and interpreting hand signals from the shunters and just as frequently stopping, starting and reversing. This is quite a tonic for pent-up boredom and a few savage attacks on a raft of wagons soon makes one feel better. Shunting is as much an art on the shunters' part as on that of the drivers. A good shunter will make as few reverses for the driver as possible, and he has a complete picture of the work required to be done.

Shunting can be likened somewhat to a game of draughts with a system for every move and a feeling of achievement on completion of the game. With forethought a good shunter saves his feet and temper. The regular driver soon knows the yard and duties as well as the shunter, and teamwork masters the job. This has one slightly unfortunate side, in that lengthy spells of inactivity can make a shift seem very long, so that it is necessary to devise something to occupy one's mind oneself. My pet occupation at this time was to clean the firebox back-plate. With the driver safely removed to the shunters' cabin for a natter, the engine was ready for operations to begin.

To start with, the cab ventilator (if fitted) and windows were opened, and a pot full of cylinder oil (pre-warmed to make it more fluid) was then trickled liberally over the back-plate and fittings. When sufficiently coated, the gauge-glasses were shut and drained and the whole scoured with the slake pipe. This operation had the effect of blacking, cleaning and lubricating. Ten minutes with a cloth would wipe off all surplus oil and dirt, and finally a good wash down resulted in a cab looking much neater and more cared for than before.

Lamps would next receive attention, with a good swill out with hot water to remove all smoke and soot. The wick would be trimmed, reflectors and glass cleaned, and the whole rubbed over with an oily cloth to produce shine. Next, the engine would receive a good oiling; finally the tools and bucket would be cleaned. If there was still time an oily rag rolled in coal dust and grit brightened up the copper pipe work and one could sit back content at having considerably improved the appearance of the cab. One rarely tried to clean the outside of the engine, for this was usually too caked with filth to warrant any such attempt. The steam brake always needed a good oiling and usually benefited, providing the lubricant did not stream out on to the ground, which, unfortunately, was often the case. Some day duties involved partial cleaning of the fire, this being usually dependent upon how long the engine had been on duty and what quality of fuel was provided.

Most of the Burton duties were connected with the brewing industry, collecting the daily output and distributing it among the various yards for despatch, and returning a balance of empties. Long before I was employed at Burton, much of the marshalling and collecting had been considerably simplified, but there still remained a large number of duties for the shunting links. Relics of earlier days still existed in the numerous yards, reminders of times when several different railways served Burton and there were many more breweries. Some of the yards were a considerable distance from the shed and entailed a lot of overtime simply in walking to and from duty. Some crews, indeed, were based at Horninglow ex-LNW shed.

Motive power for the various shunts ranged from the 0–4–0 tanks to old 3F 0–6–0s, much of the work being performed by the standard 3F 0–6–0 tanks. The 0–4–0 tanks were the smallest engines on which I had ever worked, and they were not without their problems. Their principal duty was between Shobnall Junction and down the Bond End branch. This ran at right-angles to and under the Midland main line, just south of the station. It involved quite a steep pull in either direction, owing to the dip under the main line, and with anything like a load one was usually short of 'wind' at the end of the journey. As fuel accommodation on these tanks was virtually nil, the firebox, which was quite deep, had to be well filled up with lumps to provide some lasting power. Any other fuel was carried on the tank sides and in the cab. Small wooden stages erected at various odd points supplied further coal when one was out on duty on a 'do-it-yourself' basis.

Soon I realised that to handle such a small engine economically one needed a considerable degree of skill. Without this, the tank lid was forever being opened and the fire always in need of attention. The blast on these diminutive machines was very sharp and a heavy trip or two soon emptied the firebox. Blowing-off had to be controlled to make the water go anywhere at all. On the Deeley variety, the injector water regulator ran along the top of the tanks, and as one usually stacked coal on the top of these they frequently jammed.

Compared with ordinary shunting engines the 0-4-0 tanks seemed little more than toys and were very comfortless. The earlier variety had next to no cab cover, and I often wondered how the men endured their shifts in biting winds and snowy conditions. Free cans of ale in some places were to be had at times, and doubtless helped to keep out some of the cold. The Deeley tanks had much more protection and, on hot summer days, in fact, were rather akin to heated greenhouses. Somehow, I feel little regret for the passing of these locomotives. Little engines can be every bit as difficult as big ones, though sometimes with less margin for error. Thankfully I did not often have to perform on duties involving the 0-4-0 tanks.

The 1F 0-6-0 tank was a much superior beast. Some had all-over cabs and some half-cabs; some had round-top and others Belpaire fireboxes. Whatever the difference, they performed very well and seemed little inferior to the 3F tanks.

My favourite engine was undoubtedly No 58246, an old 2F 0-6-0, with round top-firebox, Salter safety-valves and very little cab. We first worked together on the wagon works shunt near Wetmore Sidings, alongside the Tutbury line. This little darling had several peculiarities I had never met with before, including a 'spin wheel' steam brake, situated in the centre of the firebox back-plate, and a most peculiar injector, the water regulator of which operated on the tender. No slake pipe existed but a tender tap provided all necessary swilling water, heated on the blade of the shovel if necessary, for washing purposes. We spent many hours together and I took a delight in keeping her looking neat and clean. She was a lovely little steamer and could, if required, be operated by one man for hours on end. Her only fault lay in the lack of brake power, and on one occasion, when I had a raft of bolster and other heavy wagons pulling out of the wagon works rather more swiftly than usual, I had great difficulty in arresting her efforts to take to the Derby Road, which lay beyond the buffer stops.

To keep up steam it was only necessary to fill her up under the fire-door—the blast and the shunting movement took all the coal necessary to the front of the box. Her sharp blast echoed like gunshots and was usually accompanied by showers of hot sparks. I retain a very clear memory of her, silhouetted against a summer evening sky, with no trace of steam or smoke, but very much alive and belying her age. I deeply regret her passing, a grand old engine, very simple to operate and most reliable.

The only other engine types I had at Burton were 8Fs, 4Fs, 3Fs and 84XXX 2–6–2 tanks; these did not provide much variety. For a time I was in the disposal link at Burton, and it was on these duties that I first got seriously introduced to ale on the inside, and nearly with serious consequences.

I had not been at Burton very long before I had established myself as a firedropper. The day in question was hot and sunny and more than usually dusty. We had disposed of about five engines and as there was then a lull until the next arrival, it was suggested that a glass of ale would certainly go down very well indeed. I could have declined, but as this might have seemed rather anti-social I duly tagged along. On arrival at the appointed place of refreshment I was informed that this was undoubtedly the best ale brewed in the town and with that was swept into the public bar and asked for my preference. The odd bottle and shandy had been partaken in the past, but in a most modest style. After brief consideration I plumped for a small shandy and received a pint for my pains. I took a sip and reluctance soon melted into acceptance. After all, it was hot and we had had a rough day—what a jolly good idea this was! Three pints later, I felt I could 'bale out' all the Garratts at Toton, with a couple more engines as a walkover.

It was about half-way through operation on an 84XXX tank that I began to feel dizzy. Anyway, I completed the job and my mate then told me to take her into the roundhouse. As to what happened next I am not quite certain, but we hit the turntable with a resounding crash; I applied the brake with negative results, crashed her into reverse and opened her full out. Crash went the table again and we shot out of the roundhouse, over the pit and on towards the coal stage at a dickens of a pace. Still without a brake, I reversed again, got control somehow and entered the shed—now with far more caution. This time I did not use the vacuum brake, but relied on the handbrake. So much for shandies on duty! I resolved not to let this happen again and in fact almost managed to keep this resolution.

Joe, my regular mate on the shunting link, was a very dry stick indeed. We spoke hardly a word to each other for nearly a month. I had been warned that he was an old cuss, but this was hardly correct. He spoke only when in the mood and, in the early stages, more often than not he just wasn't in the mood. Gradually I became accepted and we became good friends. Joe was quiet by nature and could work a whole shift without a word. I was much the same and this understanding helped considerably. He had come originally from Wigan and appeared to have been on shunting most of his life. Few firemen liked him, partly, I believe, because of his leathery pugilistic features, but more possibly because he was not fond of larking about and was a very staid and set type of man. He was usually very clean in appearance, with neat blue overalls, suit jacket, cloth cap and well-polished boots. When in the talkative mood he was difficult to stop but very interesting to listen to, usually on any subject but railways. Over the years he had mastered the art of cooking on the engine to a fine degree and my usual complement of sandwiches and cake seemed poor stuff compared with the feasts prepared on the other side of the engine.

My first encounter with his cookery was shortly after I had become his fireman. We were on a night job and I was leaning back with one foot on the seat, eyes front and watching our shunt, when I became aware of a beautiful oniony odour. The smell of garlic to accompany an overheated big-end hardly applied to us and it took some time to realise from whence it was coming; close scrutiny of the back-plate, however, soon located the source. Neatly pushed into the hottest corners of the various pipes and fittings were about half a dozen small onions. On engines, I was informed, they would cook in their skins in about two hours or so—just in time for supper. A small basin with a muslin top rested neatly in another 'hot' corner, containing steak and kidney pie, I was told. In time I noted a variety of ways of applying heat in the interests of cookery, *via* the locomotive. Indeed, the common shovel frying was as nothing compared with this advanced art! So rapidly I terminated my supply of sandwiches and mastered the culinary art myself, with some very satisfactory results.

Rules and regulations on railways, as anywhere else, are adapted or broken at times to suit given situations. Few men abide strictly by them, so I frequently found myself in complete control of our engine—not an uncommon practice anywhere on shunting duties. As lookout the fireman is of little use, as signals are almost always on the driver's side, certainly in straight road yards. Diesel shunters are almost always single-manned, so that it was quite in order for one man successfully to manage a steam shunter. With a good fire, lasting up to an hour, and with the injector, regulator, reverse and brake on the driver's side it presented few difficulties for one man, and provided the duty was confined to one yard and involved no trip work on the main line, the practice was perfectly safe. The relieved man could then attend the local for an hour or read the paper in comfort in the cabin. It was not uncommon at times of much work for one of the engine-crew to help out on the ground, by turning points or coupling and uncoupling, this helped to speed up operations. Much time could be lost when making up fully-fitted trains and extra help was usually very welcome.

Perhaps the clearest Burton memory is the prevailing smell of malt and hops and the general odours accompanying brewing. At certain points it was stronger than at others and helped in locating oneself, especially on foggy days. Fog was as much a menace at Burton as anywhere else, but even more so. With the many different shunts and engines operated by the different brewing firms, great caution had to be taken in foggy weather to ensure safety. Rafts of wagons had an uncanny knack of appearing out of the mist with little or no warning.

Burton, however, began to depress me. I had had but two 'runs out' and was frankly fed up. Further, I was frightened I would lose touch with the job as I had certainly not bargained for continuous shunting. So I began to study the vacancy sheets again. Despite the fact that two years of army life were shortly to be my lot, I was determined that I would not return to Burton. I had made a mistake and was determined to rectify it. Several reasons had caused my transfer from Lancaster, the primary cause being that I had left home and wanted to make a really clean brake. I doubted my ability to manage top main-line work and so had shied from the biggest depots. Lodgings also worried me, and while I fancied Saltley as a base, the surrounding area did not look as though I could possibly get reasonable 'digs'. So I had settled on Burton because it was the nearest shed to Derby that had vacancies—and in Derby I had friends.

After much deliberation I decided to have a go at Crewe. Without more ado I filled in the necessary forms and let things take their own course. A few weeks before I left for the army I received notification that I qualified for one of the Crewe vacancies. This pleased me no end, as it was at least something to look forward to in the dreary months ahead.

My two years in the army were spent as a Hospital Cook, and my only firing was an occasional turn on the stationary boilers located in the hospital basement, supplying hot water and steam to the kitchen and operating theatre. The steam-raising plant comprised two Lancashire-type boilers and about four small uprights, all fired with coke. These demanded quite a different technique from locomotive boilers, and coke was the only fuel provided. To keep my hand in, I often helped out on them whilst employed as cook on night duty. My own work was usually completed by about 1am, and for most of the remainder of the night I would help out on the boiler-house duties. Much spare time was spent in studying books on the locomotive and reading about performance, also on many rail-trips and at stations watching enviously all the steam in sight. I gave much thought to my system of firing prior to going into the army and tried to work out the best way of tackling the job in future, realising that the work at Crewe would require much higher standards than those to which I had been used before.

At times I had second thoughts and regretted my decision, but these moments of doubt soon subsided. All or nothing was to be the approach; after all, big engine work was what I had always wanted, so big engine work I would have.

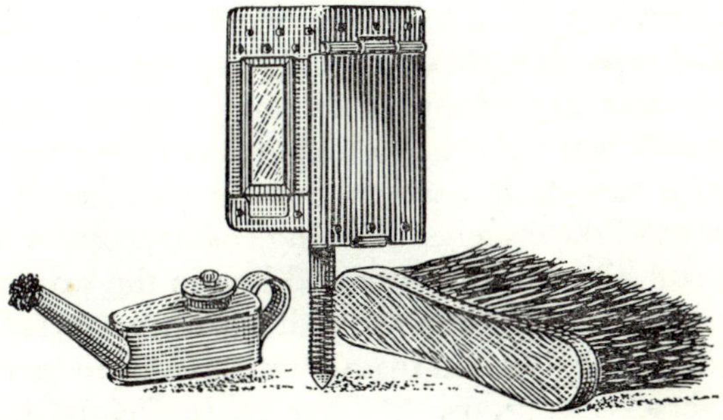

6

Introduction to Crewe

Grey, misty November weather did nothing to relieve my somewhat daunted feelings as I journeyed west from Derby to take up footplate life once more. Previous visits to Crewe had always resembled a pilgrimage to Mecca, but now thoughts of possibly being assigned to a London express the very next day produced feelings akin to stage fright. This would be a very different Crewe. No longer was I the detached enthusiast with camera and notebook in hand, plying the platforms in search of the locomotive; nor was I the traveller drinking endless cups of tea, consuming numerous pies, suffering chilly hours nodding in the waiting-rooms until the long-awaited connecting train arrived. I had transferred to the hub of the London Midland Region and from now on I was to be involved in the thick of its diverse operations. My hardly auspicious footplate career seemed totally inadequate, and my diminutive struggles of the past (albeit magnified at the time) paled before such future demands.

As things turned out my fears were unfounded, to which no doubt I owed my lack of seniority at the time, for I was initially placed on shunting turns, which enabled me to become re-accustomed to the footplate. This gentle breaking-in period was welcome indeed, and my somewhat limited experience of engine types and duties was increased in a generally painless manner.

While I could fairly claim to know Crewe as a railway centre well enough, the town itself was completely unknown to me. My initial impression was, to say the least, a depressing one. The prevailing November mist had become a fog and the mean, period architecture corresponded closely with the age of expansion of the previous century. Streets of drab little terraced houses, begrimed with soot, devoid of colour and depressingly similar, with here and there dark and forbidding chapels and old prison-like structures, the remnants of some past industry all seemed revoltingly Victorian and obsolete.

The town centre did something to correct this early reaction, but I never quite accepted the atmosphere of Crewe. Both directly and indirectly the railway had held back progress in the town, had curbed its wealth and had produced something of a monument to stagnation. But now the shackles of the past are being shaken off, and the arrears of neglect at least are being attended to. Much demolition of old property, coupled with new building, a very modern town square and a generally progressive air will, given time, do away with the accumulated squalor of the past. At the time of writing, however, this is still looking somewhat into the future. As I have said, Crewe was hardly an attractive place when I first reached it, and I was truly thankful that my job on the footplate occupied me sufficiently to be able to ignore this fact.

Administratively, the engine sheds at Crewe—North, South and, to a certain extent, Gresty Lane—were regarded as one. This meant that to all intents and purposes the North Shed was the headquarters, whence emanated all the general staff control and direction. Footplate men were separated by seniority only, the top or passenger links being based at the North Shed and the lower freight and shunting links at the South Shed. All crews, however, were well acquainted with both depots and might often find themselves booking on or off at either. In addition to regular link men, there was what was known as the 'block', a general link made up for the most part of young firemen and passed firemen (men passed to act as drivers). This general link covered the work of all links at both sheds, deputising for the regular crews' rest days, holidays and special workings, and also providing Train Control with spare sets of men to cover any unforeseen eventualities. This, broadly speaking, was the situation, save for the fact that Gresty Lane enginemen were not incorporated in the main LM staff system, retaining an element of individuality by operating only over the old GWR line to Wolverhampton. Any shortage of staff at Gresty, resulting perhaps from extra trains or rest days, was made up by the loan of staff from the 'block' link previously referred to. Enginemen for the works shunters were technically South Shed men, though they always booked on and off duty at the works, collecting their wages, as did all the staff, at the North Shed.

The sheds themselves did not differ greatly from any others, although both North and South Sheds were on the large side by shed standards and displayed a rather aged and neglected appearance. The South Shed was of much more recent origin than the North, as it had not come into being until 1897. Of rectangular construction, on the straight-road principal, it contained 12 lines, an adjacent coaling-plant and ashpit, and at its northern end a standard 70ft turntable; office and mess-room accommodation were limited only. The layout at the North Shed was very different, composed as it was of two separate but adjoining buildings with some 17 terminating roads between them. The main shed, with 12 roads, handled all the mileage examinations and heavy repairs, three or four roads being expressly reserved for this purpose. The remainder of the shed both provided shelter and undertook boiler washouts. From my own observation it would seem that, internally at least, few engines were kept in steam in the main shed, for the adjoining five-road building, devoid of any roof and known as 'Abba' (or Abyssinia), provided most of the accommodation for engines in service. All other locomotives were stabled in the open and, again from observation, this would appear to have been more than half the total operative allocation. Put another way, this meant that most of the cleaning, preparation work, oiling, coal trimming and the like, had to be carried out in the open and in all weathers. With only a limited number of outside roads possessing inspection pits, much time was wasted running about the shed looking for suitable preparing roads.

Within the area of the shed buildings lighting was particularly bad, and clambering about in the gloom on locomotives was by a sense of feel rather than by any visual means. Coupled with the poor lighting was the ever prevalent yellow smoke of freshly lit-up locomotives, which often blanketed everything in sight and reduced still further the already poor visibility. These conditions were at their worst in the early hours of the morning, when the maximum number of engines was on shed and being fired-up ready for the coming day's duty, each fire of banked-up coals being provided with the minimum of air to regulate the rise of steam pressure. At any given time several locomotives could be observed excelling themselves in smoke emission, for as their black lethargic fires were coaxed into life thick rolling clouds of smoke issued from their chimneys for perhaps half an hour. So dense was the fug at times that engines were barely visible, the only noticeable activity being the flare torches of the steamraisers going about their task. Not only was visibility impaired by the rich sulphurous cloud, but one's breathing also. Bronchially inclined myself, I noticed it perhaps more than most, suffering fits of choking and coughing which only subsided with my departure from the worst affected areas.

From within, the two buildings which comprised the North Shed appeared to have incorporated portions of much earlier establishments, with, in places, lofty stone walls, small high windows and other features suggestive of a previous existence. Successive alterations and modifications seemingly had necessitated the retention of these antique features. Personally I had the conviction that such piecemeal alteration had merely resulted in a thoroughly awkward, dismal and archaic structure quite unsuited to current needs. Although Crewe North had a progressive leaning in some directions (it possessed the first mechanical coaling-plant in the country), no one had ever been ruthless enough to completely modernise the shed, with the result that it was little more than a glorified hotch-potch, providing but poor facilities for the locomotives and even worse for the staff.

Few would dispute that coal-mining is a dirty occupation, but how many realise the degree and nature of the contamination made possible by coal dust when compounded with grease and oil? For those whose work brought them daily into close contact with the steam locomotive, filth was a word with a real meaning. For firedroppers sweating beneath layers of coal dust and ashes, begrimed cleaners, enginemen weary from hours on the footplate, fitters and the rest, filth was certainly not a joke. Whether or not the powers that be were averse to dirt being left on the premises I don't know, but there were no showers or baths provided, merely a handful of washbasins. Thus a journey home with most of the dirt still *in situ* was usual—and this often to a home of early railway origin not even provided with a bath. By contrast, lavatory facilities at the North Shed were quite reasonable, but not so at Crewe South. Here, partitioned troughs, with wooden benches and half-size doors, were thought adequate, with total exposure to the elements from above for good measure.

The mess-rooms at both sheds were literally so—they were abominable. Open vaulted roofs, dirty dishevelled walls and high dingy windows made them oppressively gloomy. Furniture was reminiscent of a junk-shop —long battered benches, and greasy-topped tables set on cracked flagstone flooring. In one corner of the North Shed mess stood a veteran gas-cooker, by the side of which, on a gas-ring, sat an almost perpetually boiling kettle—a vast black iron example, laden with scale within and cloaked with accumulated grime without. This great iron object was in constant demand, providing as it did one of the few available methods of tea brewing. At both sheds limited locker accommodation was provided—characteristically battered and forlorn, located in sometimes widely separated places, under no proper control and providing little safety for clothing and other possessions.

Both sheds possessed canteens capable of providing, at specified times, nourishing meals, and, at other times, tea and lighter fare. At the North Shed the canteen was open 24 hours a day and was most welcome for hot toast and tea, particularly on bleak, cold mornings in between shed work. Such, then, was the atmosphere of the two main Crewe sheds, the third locomotive depot to which I had been attached.

Unlike Lancaster, it is difficult to write chronologically of events at Crewe, for within a few months of shed duties and shunting, I became involved in a good cross-section of almost all types of duties worked by Crewe men. Apart from engine preparation, the other main shed job was 'taking-on'—perhaps better described as stabling. As soon as engines arrived on shed, they proceeded to be coaled and to have their fires and smokeboxes cleaned. This was the cue for my driver and myself to water the tenders, turn the engines and if necessary to place them on a suitable road for the preparing crew. This task often involved handling some 20 or more locomotives on each shift, a rate, I may add, which kept me almost continuously occupied, for it rarely took less than 20min to handle each locomotive. Co-operating on this task were outside foremen, who, on booking the engines on shed, ascertained their next duties, communicating this information to us and indicating where the locomotive was to be stabled. Adverse weather conditions, rain, snow or more particularly fog, merely added to an already difficult job, and the desire to complete one's quota of engines within eight hours indirectly was the cause of not a few collisions, derailments and similar *faux-pas*.

Two quite serious collisions occurred on one extremely foggy night, resulting in a buckled buffer-beam on one engine and a ripped tender-side on the other. During another period of fog and drizzle one of the stabling crews over-estimated the brake-power on No 45721 while they were approaching the turntable, already set for some other road, and with a rending crash the engine jack-knifed into the turntable pit, promptly disrupting the shed for the next six or seven hours. The task of removing No 45721 from the pit was, to say the least, a major one, and was further responsible for destroying a length of track to which the breakdown gang had attached a hawser for anchorage. While I do not pretend that this event was at all common, several older hands had apparently seen such capers before! These incidents, by the way, took place at the North Shed, but similar happenings were common to both sheds. Derailments were a frequent occurrence, though not usually regarded with so much amusement as when a 9F 2–10–0 (No 92016) came off the road, all wheels, at the South Shed. As the fireman on the North Shed breakdown train I had plenty of time to inspect the various manœuvres connected with its re-railing. Noticing that progress was somewhat slower than usual, I naïvely enquired of one of the breakdown crew what the trouble was. 'Matey,' he said, 'these . . . . things have too many . . . . wheels.' Point made, I thought!

Preparing engines, as it was understood at Crewe, came as something of a surprise to me, used as I was to the Midland practice of finding lamps and tools, attending to the fire and drawing the oil ration. I was, in fact, familiar with all matters other than that of oiling-up, which in the past had been strictly the driver's duty and only undertaken by me at his express wish. Crewe practice, however, required the fireman to oil the *inside* of the engine as well as doing his usual duties. Apart from the thoroughly unpleasant nature of this task, there was the added responsibility of checking that, as far as could be seen, the engine was mechanically fit for duty. Until this point in my career I had never disputed the fact that such-and-such an engine had two, three or four cylinders, plus the relevant motion, nor had I become too curious or bothered to confirm it!

Here at last my locomotive education was broadened with a vengeance! So I acquired a considerable understanding of what made multi-cylinder engines tick, or, perhaps more correctly, I became a past-master at sliding and rolling about inside engines, but only after some rather embarrassing times, tangled up amongst slide-bars, cross-heads, rockers, and all the rest. Twice I became wedged tight and once I fell out of the motion of a Princess Royal Pacific into the pit. Standing on the brake-rods and springs, or lying on top of connecting-rods was a decidedly filthy, hot and generally uncomfortable job. Various leaks of hot water trickled down one's neck from above, adding still further to the discomfort. It should be made clear that when preparing engines, speed was the order of the day. Not, I must emphasise, to the detriment of the engines concerned, but the sooner a quota of engines was completed, the sooner one went home!

Bearing in mind the shortage of roads with inspection pits, I often found it more convenient to scramble under engines on the level, sometimes much to the consternation of my driver! I say convenient, because I had no wish to waste valuable time cruising around the shed in search of a vacant pit, nor could I bother to move two or three engines which might be blocking the way—and this despite the fact that when properly set, the inside motion of an engine becomes somewhat easier to get at. And so, speed being the operative word, I put up with any amount of inconvenience rather than spend time positioning the engine. In any case, despite suggestions to the contrary, I found it possible to oil-up engines in almost any position.

Preparing engines at night time naturally was made more difficult by the almost complete lack of lighting, other than the use of a small oil torch. Balancing this, a can of oil and myself was asking for trouble. Several times I dropped the lot and torrents of curses did not, I am afraid, help matters. On one occasion, while oiling underneath an engine, another one collided (albeit slightly) with it. I have never moved so fast in all my life! Having poured oil into every cork-fitted oiling point in sight, lubricated some specialities of one's own-break pull-rods, damper levers and the injector water regulators—one had still to check for loose nuts on the eccentric straps, signs of slackening gudgeon pins, wasting white metal or excess play in the rods, broken springs, damaged water scoops and sundry other things which were not uncommon failings, despite regular engine inspection by qualified examining fitters.

An experience with No 45736 was fairly typical of this situation. She had just been returned from the works, having received a general overhaul. During preparation, the following points came to light. The brake was not functioning properly owing to a fractured steam pipe; the fire-hole ring and smoke-plate were of the wrong pattern; the cab floor-boards did not fit properly and nuts on the eccentric strap were loose. A few days after this incident, I was detailed to make ready No 45703 for a Crewe–Chester, Chester–London run. The engine had, I believe, been prepared, for I was only to coal her and spread the fire. During these manœuvres I found corks missing from the connecting and side-rods, a blow-through at a joint on the ejector steam pipe and a bad blow on the manifold. Trying the live steam injector caused clouds of steam to erupt from beneath the cab.

But now came the most frustrating part of all. I duly reported all this and qualified my report with the statement that in my opinion the engine was in no fit state to go to Chester, never mind London. Apparently nothing was done, for the next I heard of the matter the crew on No 45703 had, on arrival at the station, discovered some of these troubles and called for a fitter; the result was some 50min delay and even then a not very satisfactory engine. Fractures and blowing joints on ejector steam-pipes were rather common at this time, possibly as a result of the frosty weather, and on the same day, on being told to turn and water Pacific No 71000 we found the small ejector-pipe fractured and had to leave her for the fitters to do a brazing job.

As if the task of preparing engines to time was not thwarted enough by such troubles, the North Shed turntable broke down with alarming frequency. This entailed much working of light engines to either the South Shed turntable or the Gresty Lane triangle. Subjected to the whims of signalmen *en route*, such little jaunts were rarely completed in less than an hour.

Both sheds had considerable numbers of dead engines, which required daily manœuvring within the shed area. For this purpose a 'shop shunt' existed—one engine, crew and shunter whose job it was to drag dead engines into the fitting roads, remove repaired ones to other roads for firing up and generally to keep 'stopped' engines, as it were, on the move! The North Shed boasted two other unusual turns—the coal shunt, which kept the coaling plant topped up, at the same time disposing of the empties, and the 'Rag Mail', which wheezed to and from the works with vans of spares for the North Shed fitting shop. The coal shunt was usually worked by a 2P 4–4–0, a most unsuitable engine, which slipped and slithered and generally made very heavy weather of its task. The 'Rag Mail' turn for long was the preserve of an ex-LNW 2–4–2 tank; later an Ivatt 2–6–2 tank undertook the duty until displaced by 0–4–4 tank No 41901, an ex-Lancaster engine which revived many fond memories for me. As if the arrival of No 41901 was not enough, another old Lancaster engine, 3F 0–6–0 No 43330, had taken up its abode at the South Shed, thus doubling my pleasure.

Apart from the more normal shed work just referred to, I was occasionally assigned to other duties. The one I now describe should have been a perfectly simple operation, but owing to an unscheduled happening it became almost a disaster. I had been at Crewe for no more than a week when I was detailed to act as flagman and take an engine to the works for weighing. The engine was No 45529, and we set off, towing it through the works to the weighbridge. Everything was quite new to me, as I had never been to the works before; furthermore, I didn't really know what a 'flagman' was supposed to do. We passed the weighbridge and then set back over a pair of points and on to the line leading into it. What happened next was a bit of a mystery, for before I was fully aware of the situation, No 45529 was inside the weighhouse—unfortunately without waiting for the doors to be opened! I was frozen with terror. This, I thought, was IT. I should have to take all the blame and should probably get the sack. Almost before the sound of rending wood was over, trilby-hatted men appeared from all directions to take stock of things. I felt awful!

The actual crew who had manned the engine which towed No 45529 were familiar with the works and should, I felt, have been on the look-out. I had seen the engine being propelled slowly towards the weighbridge, expecting every minute for the brake to be applied, but only then to witness No 45529 being pushed neatly through the closed door. We had only one defence. Two metal rail checks (or straps) which should have been in position were not, but nothing else seemed to be in our favour. After a minor on-the-spot enquiry we all made our way back to the North Shed. Very little was said, though I had the uncomfortable feeling that I was hardly the most popular person at the shed.

When the time came for booking off I quite expected to be called to account for the happening, but nothing further was said of the matter and after a week or two the whole thing was forgotten. On the only other occasion on which I was 'flagman', the requirement was a little more obvious. I was sent to look after a new diesel, destined for Cardiff, and marshalled in a freight train for Shrewsbury. Having ensured that it did not run hot, I handed it and its control handle safely over at Shrewsbury, and on this occasion fortunately nothing untoward happened.

Apart from the yard trip-engines, another interesting duty was dragging engines for overhaul from the South Shed dump to the works and returning with freshly repaired ones. Both functions quite often had a common denominator in the groans of protest that one heard, in the first case because of wear and tear, and in the second because of tightness and lack of lubrication.

7

Crewe Works and Yard Shunting

Of all the duties at Crewe, nothing could challenge the works shunts for uniqueness of operation. To be employed on these duties was something completely different from any other engine duties on which I had ever been engaged previously. The works was like a separate region of BR; once inside was like being in another world; so internally self-sufficient were they. For a start, the people rostered for the works shunts booked on in the works at the same time-offices as the rest of the employees. The works staff were considerably stricter regarding time-keeping than the sheds, and they somewhat belittled the status of enginemen, as well they might. All the engines used in the works remained and were fully serviced there, only rarely proceeding to the outside world.

The size of the works was somewhat deceptive. Lack of sufficient land had resulted in the layout being confined to a comparatively narrow strip of land capable of extension lengthwise only. Successive additions had resulted in this layout becoming almost two miles long. The original shops at the eastern end had been swiftly outgrown by successive extensions and a complete network of rail connections had been built up. The principal traffic line basically followed the route of the old main line to Holyhead and Chester and was still sufficiently intact to retain an old Euston–Holyhead mile-post. To maintain this works main line and to control various works transfers a signalbox was provided.

Without wishing to be too romantic I must emphasise the prevailing Victorian-Webb atmosphere, created partially by the stern *façade* of the works offices and even more so by the tiny little rows of cottages, in some places built right up to the edge of the works. Somehow this still gave the impression of a little empire—the empire of the Webb era—and sometimes I felt certain that 'Emperor Webb' would be bound to appear in the old works *coupé*, handing out orders and commands left and right. Much of the old era remained, especially the walls of the clock tower of the old works, but also with the isolated stone buildings and abandoned sections of the once extensive narrow-gauge railway. Large sections of this remained intact, round the timber yard in particular,

The works offices were regarded with something akin to fear as one never knew who might be on the look-out for noisy or smoky engines! Further, a regiment of bowler-hatted gentlemen was continually making the rounds from this little hive, many doubtless equipped with substantial stings. Frequently a nudge from a mate would be followed by a whispered 'Pssst—that's so and so, head of this-and-that', or similar comments. A look of awesome admiration and back to the job.

So extensive was the rail system that upwards of a dozen engines were employed in various parts, together with a trip-engine feeding further engines for repairs, collected at the South Shed, and returning with alike complement, duly repaired, for trials. This engine also worked the stores vans to and from the station and South Shed with spares destined for the various motive power depots. To make matters more complex the entire system was laced with an intricate system of level crossings for the use of the employees and road tractors between the various shops. These provoked a considerable amount of whistling and clashing of hastily-braked trains making way for cross-works activities. The engines themselves added considerably to the period atmosphere. Always of ancient and quaint vintage, the contingent in my time was well up to this standard.

Large-domed and tall chimnied, LYR tender engines, venerable humpy saddle-tanks, and a brace of tiny Caledonian 'pugs', made a picturesque fleet. Several were unofficially named and I personally christened a 'Peggy' and a 'Betty'. Several were further adorned with mascots and one Belpaire boilered 0–6–0 proudly carried a lady's high-heeled shoe on the top lamp bracket—possibly the result of a scuffle on a crossing!

Though usually somewhat bedraggled and neglected one could not help but have affection for these veterans and Nos 52218 and 52464 were particular favourites of mine. As something in the nature of a treat, I presume, they periodically received new coats of black paint, but unfortunately no one kept up this smartness, and a rapid reversion to grubbiness was soon apparent. Some attention was provided in the way of repairs, but this was of a very limited nature and a trip to Horwich would have been of great benefit to the LYR stud. The prevalent excuse was always the same—'They are old engines, you know'—'bound to give trouble'—'spares very difficult now', and so on. Even if, as frequently was the case, their somewhat archaic braking system failed to act in time, resulting in violent collisions, the old excuse would be trotted out, followed, perhaps, by a consoling remark such as 'Umph . . . I'll have a look at 'er'. If it was not brake trouble, then it was injector trouble. Time and time again my thoughts strayed back to tales old 'Lanky' drivers had told me, of toiling up through Sough Tunnel on an old LYR 0-6-0 laden with coal or empties, struggling with a somewhat overheated and temperamental injector and basting it with a cold wet rag to reduce the temperature sufficiently to get it to work again, while at the same time smothering the face with another wet rag to keep out the choking smoke and fumes. Injector trouble was most likely to occur when the level of the tender had got to about one-third of the capacity. The injector delivery pipe up the firebox back-plate would become unbearably hot and nothing short of a cold tank of water would really cure it.

On a couple of occasions we had to drop the fire because of this, and because all roads to the nearest water-column in the works were blocked, panic ensued. Rapid paddling of a hot fire, and anxious glances at both the bottom nut and in the firebox to see how the lead plug was behaving, was accompanied by a heated conference with the shunters to clear a road to the 'pump'; all felt mighty gallant in the face of a possible explosion—or so we thought!

Considering the very heavy nature of the works shunting, often hauling five or six engines or a train of boilers, the old-timers did surprisingly well and were quite sure-footed. This was just as well, for sand was only delivered by a complicated two-handed action—operating a release lever and feeding cupfuls of sand from the sand-boxes in the cab down a delivery pipe; human mechanisation was what we called it.

Another feature somewhat peculiar to the works was the very respectable state of the fireman. Gay shirts and well-groomed hair seemed the order of the day. This, I discovered, was because of the existence of a considerable number of pretty young typists and girl messengers. They were regarded as very good sport, and many and peculiar were the antics performed to attract their attention. Not a few blushing maids were seen pursued by a whistle-popping engine amidst great laughter from all around and to increase their rate of travel the cylinder cocks were sometimes opened as well.

Yard shunting turns

As the junction of six important traffic routes, the site of extensive marshalling yards and numerous groups of sidings, as well as a cattle market and a tranship warehouse—not to mention local coal sidings—Crewe was the centre of much shunting and trip working. Apart from continuous marshalling operations in the Basford yards, where diesel shunters held all but full sway, the remaining duties were still the province of steam. The engines were usually of Midland extraction, 2F 3F and 4F tender engines and 3F tanks.

At one time or another I believe I sampled all the various local turns and in consequence gradually succeeded in unravelling the complex mass of lines in the Crewe area. To the lay observer, shunting operations probably appear as the least adventurous of enginemen's duties and at most times they were, but they nevertheless still deserve some attention, if only to show how difficult things could become.

I was assigned to a week's work on the wagon shop shunt, where activities were centred on a yard adjacent to the Shrewsbury or Gresty line For the first two days we were provided with an old MR 2F goods, No 5.8196. This little charmer suffered from a multitude of ailments. The injectors only partially worked and wasted about as much water as they put into the boiler. The ejectors were in a very poor state and it required the large one to be on continuously to make 21in of vacuum. The persistence of these two ailments necessitated our frequent attendance at the water column. The piston glands blew so badly that shunting operations were conducted in a permanent fog. Sanders did not function and a frosty rail provided prolonged periods of 'running on the spot', much to the chagrin of our shunter. The fire was blue, the brick arch falling in, and the only fuel provided was briquette dust. These factors combined to make the operation of the wagonshop shunt something of a nightmare instead of the sober little effort it should have been. Crisis point was reached with our one big effort of the shift.

Apart from rearranging the shop roads, removing the wagons which had received attention and pushing others into their place, we had to collect the days supply of damaged and otherwise unusable wagons from the siding near the tranship shed. This necessitated running down a steep little incline which, with anything like a load, meant a short but severe pull back to the wagon shops. One day, as luck would have it, 35 mainly loaded wagons required attention. With much effort I coaxed No 58196 into some sort of order suitable for such a bid, and with the blower hard on, plenty of steam, smoke and clanking we set sail in full forward gear and hoped for the best. We did not run up the bank; it was one prolonged slip. Even so we managed to get about half-way up when signals intervened—a main-line freight, making up its train in the top end of the warehouse yard, straddled right across our path. When the signals eventually favoured us I am afraid nothing else did; we couldn't budge an inch and so our train had to be divided.

By this time our fire was a variegated mass of blues, greens and purples, with deep, black furrows and very little heat-producing matter. The tender was one mass of wet, grey dust and I was cold, dusty and fed up. It was infuriating that one insignificant little shunting duty could provide so much trouble! More of the brick arch had fallen and my fire-irons were soft, twisted and useless after vain attempts to keep the fire bright. How glad I was to drop on to South Shed and leave that little horror behind there! The remainder of the week was distinctly more favourable. Standard 3F tanks in much better order and much less work made for a more enjoyable time; in fact, there was so little to do that I spent much time in a nearby pub or in the mess-room at the GWR shed, talking shop.

Another ridiculous affair took place in North Staffordshire on the 'Knotty' yard, with No 47680. The engine had half its brick arch down and was steaming very poorly; soon the rest fell in and we discovered a nest of 12 leaking tubes. In addition, the regulator gland was leaking like a miniature waterfall. There was nothing else for it—we went off to shed and were signed off. Not all shunts, of course, were as ill-starred as this, though they were often beset by little troubles of various kinds. When winter set in conditions could be appalling—points frozen or jammed with snow were matters usually taken in one's stride but at times things became too much. . . .

Some of the worst conditions I can recall occurred on three consecutive days when working the 'Knotty' trip (from North Stafford sidings to Basford Hall sidings). Snow had been falling intermittently for several days and had become quite deep; in addition it was bitterly cold and visibility was poor. Trip working between yards in these conditions could be very miserable. In our particular state they became absolutely awful. Our engine, 4F No 44186, had been on duty 24 hours continuously and her fire was deep with clinker. Long runs with coal from the NS section to Basford Hall yards, conducted mainly over a steep connecting incline, required considerable effort, hampered as we were with these arctic conditions, poor visibility and little steam. Part way through the first day a near blizzard was experienced and the tarpaulin cover stretched from the cab top to the front of the tender broke loose and required anchoring. All the time thick driving snow swept through the cab from side to side. The yards south of Crewe were very exposed and, in conditions such as these, a place from which it was better to keep as far away as possible! Blue with cold, wet and miserable, plus a temperamental fire requiring constant darting and breaking up, coupled with delays owing to clogged points, cut off from boiling tea water (this in itself constituting a crisis of the first magnitude) by a deep carpet of snow which hid the numerous 'bear traps' so common in large yards—points, rods and wires, rails, sleepers and unknown piles of spoil left by the last permanent way effort—made the eight hours drag on interminably.

The second day was equally horrible and at one point we just had to make some tea or freeze to death. I only succeeded in doing so after three nasty falls, owing to my not having been aware of 'bear traps' until it was too late. A cut hand and a grazed knee, soaked shoes and socks, wet trouser bottoms—these were all earned on behalf of that can of tea. The engine was the same as the previous day and had not returned to shed in between. The fire was in dire straits and, in fact, only after I had paddled out about a dozen or so shovelsful of clinker was there any room for anything else under the arch. The tender contained no more than a frozen grey-white powder, attached firmly to the top and sides with ice and snow and only removable by repeated attacks with the coal pick.

Our endeavour to take water met with a fate almost worse than death itself. On reaching the ice rink at the back of the tender (an ascent, I might add, undertaken in a very gingerly fashion), I found the tank lid firmly bonded to the aperture. Repeated blows with the coal pick disposed of this little obstacle, but our troubles, I am afraid, were only just beginning. The leather delivery pipe connection was found to be frozen solid, despite a brazier of hot fire placed near by. Even during less frigid times six feet of stout leather was a difficult thing to handle and in these conditions it was the very devil! The coal pick was again brought into use and an element of flexibility induced after some considerable belabouring. Having heaved the slab of frozen leather on to the tender the water was turned on. At first nothing happened; then, suddenly, an enormous swelling appeared and before steps could be taken to release it a violent and considerable deluge resulted in two drenched enginemen retreating to the comparative warmth of a miserable cab to consult as to what should be done next.

As my driver was the more soaked, it was decided that he should suffer a further drenching and shut off the cascade. This done, I returned to the back of the tender, almost slipping off in my attempt, and delivered a further series of blows to the leather monster. Large pieces of ice were dislodged, and with the flow of water restored a supply at last entered the tank. While we were thus engaged, a particularly thick fog had developed. Everything became still, quiet and fathomless, and as we could no longer judge distances, further work became impossible. The Shunters had retreated to their respective cabins and we were left to fend for ourselves. To continue was out of the question and there was nothing else for it but to beat a retreat to the shed. This could only be accomplished at less than a walking pace, and with myself about 20ft ahead, signalling with a headlamp.

The third day was similar, though without another water-column experience; the fire was so bad, however, that it had to be thoroughly cleaned; its mixture of briquettes and dirt simply ran on the bars. As a finale, we were unable to place our engine on the disposal road at the shed without first moving some half a dozen others. During this operation I badly jammed my thumb on the reversing lever of No 43330 and walked

Class WD 2–8–0 No 90441 on the 15.15 Perth–Thornton Junction freight at Hilton Junction in August, 1965 *D. A. Idle*

Patriot 4–6–0 No 45510 on a morning Carnforth–Leeds semi-fast leaving Hellifield *Derek Cross*

A southbound fitted freight on Dillicar troughs headed by Patriot 4-6-0 No 45551 in July 1961 *Derek Cross*

Jubilee 4-6-0 No 45626 Seychelles on the Midland main line between Carlisle and Cumwhinton with the 14.39 Carlisle–Leeds freight in October 1964 *Peter J. Robinson*

Three views of the triple accident at Basford Hall in November 1958

Macdonald & Good

Royal Scot 4–6–0 No 46132 *The Kings Regiment Liverpool* **takes the through road from the south at Crewe with the down 'Red Rose' in July 1959** *T. Lewis*

Royal Scot Class 4–6–0 No 46155 *The Lancer* **at Patricroft m.p.d. in October 1962** *J. R. Carter*

home in a snowstorm, feeling very tired, very cold and anything but happy.

About this time, I had, for a short period, my one and only regular driver at Crewe. All my other work was usually performed with a different mate each day or, at most, for a week's work only. This driver was a remarkable man, whose life centred around gambling and cards, while horses were his speciality. He was the only successful gambler I have ever met and horses usually kept him in pocket, come the end of the week, while his skill at cards was little short of amazing. He was comparatively well-off, owning a large house, of which, I believe, a few rooms were let out. On the whole I got on quite well with this cheerful, chirpy personality. There was, however, one slight source of friction, and this developed during a spell with 0–6–0 No 43562. She had recently been through shops and was in beautiful condition. From the first day I had her, I could not resist 'blacking her front' and polishing up the various cab fittings. Many times, I worked on her, taking considerable pride in her. Being so recently overhauled she was a beauty, sound as a bell and with a tight front-end and hardly a knock. Everything worked properly and she was a real joy to work on.

By my mate my cleaning efforts were regarded as curious, to say the least. As far as he was concerned engines were started and stopped and that was about all there was to it. He himself was usually smart and clean in appearance, and he preferred as little contact as possible with the oil-can. I, on the other hand, spent a considerable amount of time cleaning and oiling and generally attending to footplate duties. He would fill the box up, adjust the dampers, read his paper and perhaps drop off for a natter or a game of cards. As soon as we had stopped he was all for roping me in on a hand of cards. This I declined, however, owing to the fact that I had to clean and oil up, something which I told him I felt he ought to be doing. This didn't go down at all well and a rift developed between us which was never really healed.

In general, the condition of Crewe shunting locomotives was rather poor. Their problems were twofold—overwork and old age, the elderly MR 2F 0–6–0s suffering in particular. By this latter I do not wish to convey pictures of panting, wheezing, senile 0–6–0 tanks sagging at the wheels, but rather one of their being kept in traffic almost continuously; consequently small repairs were neglected until they assumed greater significance. Twenty-four-hour shunts were a regular feature to which they did not take kindly. The high mileage run up by these engines and others between shoppings—so gushingly cited by BR and various journals in past years—was, in my view, highly detrimental to them. The most common ailments arising from this practice are typified by my experience on Nos 58196 and 47680. After not much more than 12 months from the shops and notwithstanding shed repairs and maintenance, tanks leaked, severe play developed in the motion, and the tyres, brake and injector equipment deteriorated badly. The boiler, too, did not escape as stays and tube-plates leaked and smokebox doors became warped. The fuel supplied was often of the poorest quality, much slack swept from the tenders of engines 'in for shopping' finding its way into the bunkers! Despite the illusion that anything would do for shunting, this just was not so and resulted in much wasted time and effort, as well as dictating the need for detrimental forcing measures when we were handling the engines concerned.

Among the very mixed bag of engines that Crewe retained for shunting was No 47280, peculiar in that, like No 47201 at Lancaster, the sand-boxes were filled from above the tank top. The majority of LMS-built 3F tanks, however, had recessed boxes in the tank sides which one filled with the aid of a funnel. The position of the sand-boxes (or, rather, their filling point) made necessary the humping of sand-buckets 'upstairs' as it were, first from ground level to the frames, followed by a swift vertical snatch and, with a bit of luck and some spillage, the bucket at last reached its destination.

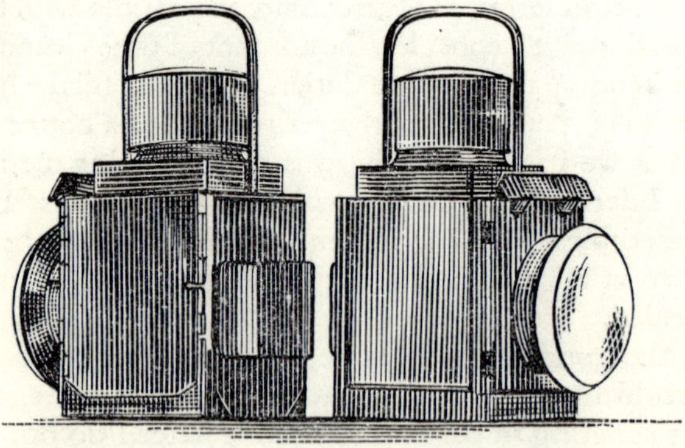

8

Lines out of Crewe

The great variety of work at Crewe, much of it over scattered and contrasting routes, compensated to a large extent for the more tedious aspects of life there. It must be admitted, however, that while much of the work did not allow much time for admiring buttercups and daisies, some of the short-distance runs over lines such as those to Shrewsbury and Manchester did allow time enough, in between rounds, to absorb some of the beauties of the countryside. The Shrewsbury line (or 'Salop line' as we called it) to my mind was the most attractive of the shorter routes worked over by Crewe men, with its pretty undulating stretches offering occasional peeps of the black-and-white houses characteristic of the area.

Shortly after leaving Crewe one passed through Nantwich—surely one of the most attractive towns in Cheshire, with its early buildings and architectural interest. Two level crossings intersected the railway at Nantwich, causing much delay, especially to freight trains. Just beyond Nantwich the line climbed over the Shropshire Union Canal, and thence up the formidable $7\frac{1}{2}$-mile climb past Wrenbury, much of it at between 1 in 97 and 115 in grade. At Whitchurch, the destination of works trial runs for new and repaired engines, the Cambrian's Oswestry line was joined and also the Tattenhall–Chester branch. Over the former came the occasional Western Region Manor class 4–6–0s to Crewe on freight trains, and there was also much activity at Whitchurch in the shape of WR 22XX type 0–6–0s and LMR Ivatt type 2–6–0s.

When passenger service over the Tattenhall branch came to an end the independent locomotive shed at Whitchurch was closed, and some of its staff were transferred to Crewe for more exacting duties, causing no little friction because it became necessary to absorb some quite senior men into the top links. Already at an advanced age, these stalwarts (whose footplate experience had often not advanced beyond the limits of a 2P 4–4–0) in some cases found themselves heading for the Border on a Duchess Pacific. Many were the tales about this time of violently slipping 4–6–2s, of lost time and of steam shortage, all attributed to these newcomers. Some of them never got further than attempts at learning the road, and were defeated by the welter of signals, junctions and the like on the main line north of Crewe. However, this is a digression. The Tattenhall line provided Crewe with a pick-up freight to Broxton which started at Crewe and shunted and sorted goods at Nantwich, Wrenbury and Whitchurch before taking to the branch, calling at Malpas, *en route* to Broxton. There a prolonged break usually ensued before the train returned to Whitchurch and home.

Beyond Whitchurch the main line continued through a generally agricultural scene, passing Prees, Wem, Yorton and Hadnall before finally approaching Shrewsbury on a steep down grade and around a very sharp curve into the station. Locomotive work over the line, with stiff gradients and curves, was quite exacting, especially for passenger trains with their tight schedules. Loose-coupled freight workings were made more difficult by the frequent dips in the line causing, if one were not careful, 'snatch' in the couplings with the risk of a break-away. Much of the through freight on this line consisted of steel girders and rails between South Wales and the North-East of England. Through trains were normally powered by LMR locomotives, but at times of engine shortage, WR engines continued on from Shrewsbury through to Crewe. One night two WR Castle class 4–6–0 engines appeared on successive passenger trains at Crewe.

Next to the Salop line, the Manchester road was the most interesting. I had used it often when at school as a child in Wilmslow, and in consequence I knew much of the surrounding countryside quite well, particularly that of the very beautiful Alderley Edge and Styal districts. This period spent at Wilmslow reminds me of what is perhaps a very little known 'railway'. The school paid a visit to Crewe Hall, where a chemical company had its headquarters. Having inspected the various products of the place we were shown round the Hall itself. Somewhere beneath the main dining-room, in a sort of tunnel, was a goodly length of what, from memory, must have been broad-gauge track, running from the kitchens to lifts below the dining-rooms. Whether any form of motive power was used, other than human propulsion, I am not sure, though I believe that horses were mentioned. I have often wondered since whether Crewe Works had in some way been connected with the installation.

The Manchester line between Crewe and Sandbach was notable because of the subsidence caused by underground salt workings. So bad had this sinking become that ordinary ballast was replaced by loads of clinker, a more economic method in the circumstances. Sandbach, famous for its association with the salt industry, served as a cross-roads for the important lines connecting the Midlands with the Wirral, running from near Alsager and the Potteries lines by way of Hassall Green, Sandbach and Middlewich and branching off at Northwich to the Helsby and Hooton areas. Beyond Sandbach the Manchester line became rural until Alderley Edge and Wilmslow heralded the outer conurbation of Mancheser, with a growing density of houses from Cheadle Hulme onwards. At Wilmslow the Styal loop line, avoiding the Stockport bottleneck, headed off to the left. Near Holmes Chapel the massive radio telescope at Jodrell Bank dominated the landscape, and even in the foggiest conditions served as a landmark for engine-crews, something of a reversal of its intended function, no doubt!

Stockport was the relieving point for many of the freight workings from Crewe, destined as most were for Yorkshire terminals. Beyond Stockport the line proceeded through a built-up area including some stations whose architecture suggested that they had enjoyed a charmed life. Manchester, so far as I was concerned, meant London Road Station, always an interesting place with glimpses of ex-Great Central and London & North Eastern locomotives and an atmosphere of general activity and bustle. To me, some terminals seemed forbidding and unattractive, and urged me to retire with all possible speed (Birkenhead Woodside, for instance). But not so London Road. I enjoyed all my visits there and regretted it when the time came for departure. The Manchester line was as level as made no odds, and consequently the work over it was what we called a 'doddle', it presented no difficulty whatsoever, and a few good rounds of coal sufficed for the 30-mile run.

I wish that I could enthuse in the same manner about the Northwich and Stoke lines, but they had little or no appeal to me. Of the former the less said the better. I was destined to endure frequent turns on the 'Salt Expresses' over this line, manning 4F 0–6–0s on sometimes exceedingly heavy trains. Whatever the prevailing weather conditions the Northwich line remained drab and unappealing. In matters of vegetation, the line was unaffected by the seasons, the salt and chemical refuse associated with it having killed much of nature's efforts, allowing a sort of chemical poison to grip the area. One bright feature was Middlewich station, attractively and amusingly decorated by, I believe, the signalman. A garden of sorts, with curious animal ornaments concocted out of such things as old motor-car tyres and rubber hose, was quite a welcome relief to the otherwise all-pervading drabness. The line was heavily graded and was single-tracked from Middlewich to Northwich. Local traffic, much of which consisted of salt, had declined somewhat over the years in favour of road transport. When the local push-and-pull passenger service from Crewe to Northwich ceased, all that remained, apart from the through traffic to the Wirral, were local parcel trains and pick-up freights.

Whenever one was booked to work on the line to Stoke, the usual reference was to 'working up the Pots'. Crewe steam turns over this route usually terminated somewhere in the vicinity of Stoke. Occasionally, however, special trains (often steam substitutes for failed diesel railcars) worked right through to Derby. The 'Pots' line seems, on reflection, to have been reasonable enough itself, but the secondary nature of the duties over this route brought it into disfavour. Such was the dawdling and dithering around Alsager, followed by a visit to every siding and loop between Chatterley and Stoke, that these turns were best described as main-line shunts. Another doubtful feature of these workings was their short duration, rarely occupying the full eight-hour shift, and usually culminating in one having to prepare a few engines on return to Crewe. The not infrequent contacts with Stoke and Alsager engines was always something of a hazard, for they were invariably dubious steamers and occasionally declined to steam altogether. Knowledge that this was a hard water district did nothing to relieve my aversion to this section and I retained a deep-seated feeling that, boiler scale or not, strange things were done to the engines at their home sheds.

Geographically speaking, the 'Pots' line divided itself neatly into three distinct divisions. That from Crewe to Harecastle was a pretty section of the line, well wooded and unspoilt save for a munitions factory at Radway Green, near Alsager. Harecastle Tunnel, which neatly marked the boundary of the second, or Stoke section, was approached by an up gradient through Kidsgrove and was the most repugnant of 'holes' I ever had to experience. I had always felt that Thackley Tunnel, near Leeds, was an unholy place, but Harecastle was even worse being longer and with cascades of ice-cold water percolating through the tunnel roof and adding to an already bitterly cold atmosphere. I once journeyed its length running tender first on an LNW 0–8–0 and felt I had been not far short of freezing to death!

The eastern side of Harecastle Tunnel opened, as it were, on to a different world, of collieries, chemical plants, potteries, iron and steel, and sundry concentrated industries—a scene which persisted through Longport, Etruria and Stoke to beyond Longton. However, this scene was not without its beauty when seen from the footplate at night, for immediately on leaving the tunnel a scene of fairy-like grandeur presented itself, with countless furnaces giving off multi-coloured flames and volcano-like eruptions, the like of which in such profusion I have never seen elsewhere. In such a setting the 'Pots' had, perhaps, its compensations.

The last division started near Longton, with the line climbing steeply out of the Potteries basin almost to Blythe Bridge, and continuing amid pleasant countryside to Uttoxeter, with its station situated on two faces of a triangle of lines. These led to the Churnet Valley and to Buxton. Beyond, the railway, for much of the way accompanied by the pleasant River Dove, continued through Sudbury, Tutbury and Egginton Junction, to join the Derby–Birmingham main line at Stenson Junction. It was only rarely, however, that I worked as far as Derby, for along with other Crewe men I was usually relieved at Stoke, in a similar way to the frequent practice at Rugby and Carnforth. Such were barriers indeed, where throngs of relief engine-men made further progress almost impossible!

North-west from Crewe lay Chester, and from there the lines to Birkenhead, Mold Junction and various points through to Holyhead. Turns to Holyhead were sparse and rather regretfully I never proceeded beyond Llandudno. As far as Chester the line was similar in many respects to the Shrewsbury road, though by comparison almost dead level. Attractive Cheshire country was in view for most of the way, with Beeston Castle on its hill, a celebrated local beauty spot, situated about half-way. Adjacent to much of the line was the Shropshire Union Canal, the banks of which, particularly in the summer, acted as host to numerous anglers. On hot sultry days I would watch them from the cab, envious of their peaceful little world, so remote from the rigours of life aboard an engine.

Chester I found a fascinating and attractive place, the station itself having much the same appeal for me as Manchester London Road. Whenever possible I made a point of looking around the decrepit ex GWR engine-shed, situated just to the west of the station, and thanked my lucky stars for the small mercies of Crewe, primitive though the Crewe sheds were. For one reason or another, Great Western moves to replace their venerable structure with a more modern one at Green Lane, Saltney, were frustrated. The Chester LMR shed, on the other hand, though a fairly conservative affair was at least of modern design.

From Chester the old Birkenhead Joint line proceeded north via Hooton and Bebington, terminating (if that be the right description) in the mass of lines around Birkenhead Woodside. The line had little to excite comment, save for the joint nature of the engine-sheds at Birkenhead where, as at Shrewsbury, the contrasting Western and London Midland images became readily apparent. Always on the look-out for the unusual, I delighted in the sight of the WR 47XX 2–8–0s, some of which were shedded at Birkenhead. Peculiar to the Birkenhead road, as if to compromise with the WR, was the extensive use on both passenger and freight trains of the Stanier 2–6–0s. Why this was so I never discovered, but this line and the line to Mold Junction was decidedly home territory to many of the class.

On the main line, shortly after leaving Chester, Mold Junction is reached, but as the Mold area had for me the same lack of appeal as the Northwich line, I do not propose to dwell on it, other than to express my thankfulness at being able to pass it by. The engines stationed here suffered badly from the local hard water, though unlike the Stoke area engines, they did not seem to suffer so much in respect of their steaming abilities.

Much Crewe work beyond Mold Junction took place during the summer months; it consisted mainly of summer holiday trains, usually destined for Rhyl and Llandudno. For 32 miles from Mold Junction this line was almost level, and one could work up some spectacular speeds without much effort. Most of the special trains were in the charge of Class 5s, and they were ideal. A good fire, made up when leaving Chester, needed but little attention to take one to either destination, and provided the fireman with plenty of opportunity to put his feet up on the oil cupboard and to enjoy the ride. The little humps at Queensferry and Connah's Quay were great fun. Given a clear road one could work up sufficient speed to feel literally floating on air for a second. Another source of entertainment was provided by greatly increasing the noise of the engine's exhaust when approaching the caravan sites which flanked much of the line. This would usually cause the campers to rush to the lineside to see our engine going all out, cinders and smoke streaking high into the sky. The approach from Abergele to Colwyn Bay has a short climb at 1 in 100 to Llysfaen, followed by a drop through Penmaenrhos tunnel. So high were speeds on this line that often sheer momentum was enough to take one right up the bank and down into Colwyn. One major attraction of the coast-line runs, was the inviting blue sea, though, contrasting with the dust and heat of the footplate, it offered a strong temptation to abandon the engine and join the holiday-makers!

From the delight of the North Wales coast the next lines to be considered are those to Liverpool and Birmingham. I did relatively little work over either route, but enjoyed from time to time their added variety. The Liverpool workings became interesting from Weaver Junction onwards. The final 1 in 100 of Birdswood bank, which starts just after leaving the junction, could be a stiff proposition, for the junction precluded anything in the nature of a really fast approach. With heavy tanks trains I had many anxious moments, though with no shortage of steam. But from about midway up the bank speed was often so low that the engine became smothered under a cascade of cinders exhausted at little short of full-gear. In the opposite direction a similarly steep incline, 4 miles at 1 in 115, provided a similar problem from Ditton Junction through Runcorn to Sutton Weaver. If one was making for Liverpool with a loose-coupled goods, extreme caution with the brake was needed all the way down this bank. Once over Runcorn Bridge, that glorious latticed structure which rattled and shook with every turn of the wheel and down to Ditton Junction, the line was level enough to cause no further trouble. Beyond lay Speke Junction shed, with Garston Docks in the background, the starting point of many banana specials. The line continued on through Allerton and

Wavertree, where freights headed for Edge Hill and passenger trains went down the 'hole' to Lime Street. With the Mersey and its associated industries, marine activities and vast, sprawling housing estates, it was certainly a line full of interest and no little excitement.

The Birmingham lines, in common with those to Liverpool, seemed somewhat divorced from the main line proper. By this I mean that no matter how well laid and constructed, or how busy, these lines had an importance that was secondary to those to London, Carlisle and Scotland. This impression was magnified to Crewe men by the comparatively short distance to either place. The Birmingham lines proper may be said to begin at Stafford, climbing steadily at around 1 in 330–460 through Penkridge to Bushbury. From there, two routes onwards to Birmingham New Street station could be used, either via Bescot and Aston or via Wolverhampton High level and Smethwick. Several other approaches to New Street were possible, but with the possible exception of the Walsall line, I doubt whether many Crewe men were acquainted with these roads. As it was, the two routes we frequently used were complicated enough, with their profusion of signals and junctions.

To me the Birmingham area had to be viewed in relation to the work we usually performed. Most of my work to Birmingham was on through expresses from Liverpool or Manchester, which we re-manned at Crewe. With the exception of the London runs and the Crewe-worked South Wales expresses to Shrewsbury, they were the fastest-timed duties we had. With a quick turn round at Birmingham they gave 'little time to savour the surroundings. Near Wolverhampton High Level Station one had a splendid bird's-eye view of the once grand Stafford Road Works of the old Great Western, often displaying a fair cross-section of WR engine types in various stages of repair. Bescot and Ascot engine-sheds were usually worth a passing glance, as they often were host to quite unusual and interesting locomotives. New Street itself left me with rather mixed impressions, somewhat dependent on the end from which I entered it. Often in the approach to New Street I seemed to lose my bearings. If anything, this station displayed too much bustle, and at night-time it played host to some of the more unsavoury elements of Birmingham!

Last of all we come to the West Coast main line proper, which is too well known to need much detailed description. This is just as well, for a coverage in detail of the entire route between Euston, Crewe, Carlisle, Glasgow and Perth would be beyond me. Not only were the long-distance runs on the footplate too exacting to allow of much attention to the line, but so far as I was concerned they were too infrequent to allow me to form any definite opinions. However, apart from the long-distance journeys to and from Carlisle and beyond, there was plenty of work over this line to places less distant, such as turns northwards to Warrington, Wigan, Preston and Carnforth, and southwards to Stafford, Nuneaton and Rugby.

As previously mentioned, firing northwards from Crewe was easier than that to the south. From Crewe there were slightly falling grades most of the way to Warrington, apart from the Ship Canal flyover; beyond Warrington the short climb to Golborne Junction was not difficult and from there another favourable stretch continued to Wigan, whence, but for the sharp climb to Coppull, there were few further obstacles to Carnforth. From Carnforth in the reverse direction the climb out of Lancaster was the first formidable gradient, with collar-work resumed after Preston, up to Coppull, and, later, the Ship Canal flyover once again. There were usually sufficient signal checks coming south to prevent anything in the way of fast running. Some freight workings over this section were diverted at Standish via the Whelley line, which by repute was very difficult, with stiff gradients. No doubt I was fortunate in never having to sample the delights of this diversionary route.

From Crewe to the Ship Canal the West Coast main line ran through a mainly agricultural scene, but this terminated abruptly at Warrington, where the industrial image took over and persisted most of the way to Preston. Warrington presented a flourishing picture, with thriving manufacturing works and an air of wellbeing. From about Golborne onwards, however, the Wigan coal-field dominated the scene to beyond Coppull, with vast slag heaps and desolate expanses reminiscent of past colliery activities, for in the vicinity of the line most of the collieries seem to have been worked out and those near Coppull were mere shells of their former importance. Much mining still persisted in the Wigan area, however, and the enormous sidings near Springs Branch Junction were usually full of coal trains. An LNWR flavour persisted here until the late 1950s, in the shape of numerous ex-LNW 0–8–0 goods engines which seemed to infest the area. Prior to their demise, the eight-coupled tank version of the tender engines found a home here amid the vast marshalling yards.

Always worth a look when passing through Wigan was the ex-LYR low-level station, in the yard of which one could often see an example of the once numerous Fowler 0–8–0s which in turn had ousted the last of the LYR 0–8–0s. These appeared to wait here ready to assist freights up the connecting line from the low-level to the LNW line. Past Coppull and on to Leyland the line ran parallel to the vast Leyland Motors concern, after which came Farington Junction, where usually an ex-LYR 0–6–0 from Lostock Hall could be seen performing. Just south of the overbridge at Preston were Ribble sidings, relief point for not a few of our northbound freights. Beyond Preston the scenery reverted to rural conditions and a near level line all the way to Oubeck box, then dropping down into Lancaster and over the Lune viaduct, after which it skirted the coast past Hest Bank to Carnforth, another point where many of our turns were relieved. All northbound freights leaving Crewe avoided the station by the underpass; pulling out of this up the 1 in 100 gradient with a heavy train soon enlivened an engine's fire.

Southwards from Crewe trains were immediately faced with the 10-mile climb to Whitmore. The line was quadrupled as far as Stafford and was the scene of not a few friendly races between trains on the fast and slow roads, terminated often by adverse signals, usually for the slow road competitor, at the approach to Stafford. Once past Stafford, Shugborough tunnel led to the long and nearly level stretch through the Trent Valley, and the easily-graded continuation on to Nuneaton and Rugby. The gradients met with on this route were roughly the same in each direction. So much by way of introduction to my footplate runs from Crewe.

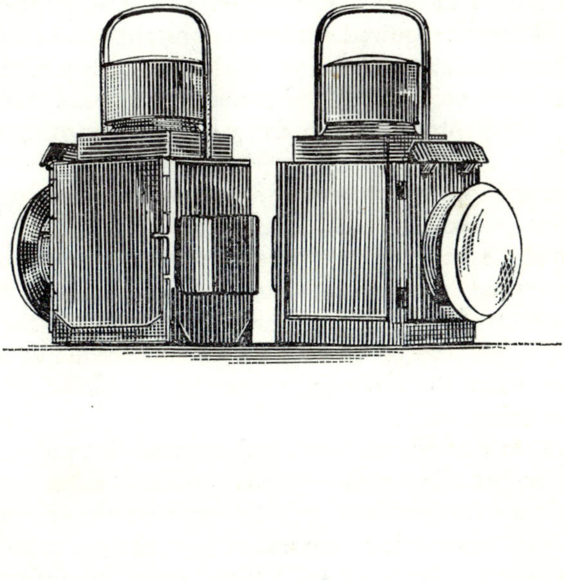

9

Footplating on the Main Line

Crewe is, of course, mainly associated with duties on the West Coast main line, serving as a very important dividing point between the fast running section to and from Euston and what at this time was the somewhat more easily timed section northwards. When my West Coast experiences began, as a personal choice I always preferred the latter, for despite obstacles like the climbs to Shap and Beattock, the pace was steadier and more to my liking. South of Crewe required an almost constant rate of firing, allowing little or no let-up from start to finish. With the gentle undulations of this line there were no stretches over which the engine could really be eased.

But despite the problems south from Crewe, returning from Euston could be a nightmare. The trouble was Camden—or rather the stringent ruling with regard to the emission of smoke there—and negligent steam-raisers. To emit smoke at Camden was a dreadful crime, carrying a most severe reprimand. Local residents keenly observed the atmosphere prevailing over the shed, and the first sign of a 'dirty' chimney resulted either in direct complaints or, perhaps worse, a complaint to the hierarchy at Euston. Being fully aware of this, I found extreme difficulty in preparing a sufficiently good fire to tackle the severe climb out of Euston and the collar-work to Tring summit.

Had the fire on our engine been well burned through matters would have been easier, but the steam-raisers at Camden had a dreadful habit of filling the firebox with coal just prior to one's arriving for a job, thereby making it almost impossible to have a well-burnt fire on leaving Euston. Efforts to cure the smoke problem in the shape of allowances of 'coalite' for lighting-up purposes had, to my mind, a detrimental effect on the firebed, which then had insufficient 'body' to make steam at the rate required when leaving Euston. As if these troubles were not enough, the boilers of engines at Camden were frequently too full, allowing no room for keeping the engine quiet while the fire was burning up.

Imagine, if you can, this typical experience. We had a Royal Scot and over 400 tons to work to Crewe, with one stop at Rugby. On arrival at the engine it would be to find over 200lb of steam on the 'clock', a full boiler and a mass of coal lumps in the firebox with barely a glimmer of fire. Without making any smoke or permitting prolonged blowing-off from the safety-valves one had to arrive at Euston with a well-burned-through fire and a full head of steam. In such conditions this would be hardly possible, and it would be touch-and-go with steam and water to Tring, dropping a few minutes in the process and with no let-up down to Bletchley—in fact, it would be hard going all the way to Kilsby Tunnel. After this, with luck, the engine could coast into Rugby, and with a little pulling round with the jet and the injector hard at work, one might be able to depart in better shape for the sprint up the Trent Valley.

Even with favourable conditions, express duties from Euston were exacting and required hard work as round by round one trimmed the coal forward, cracked it up, fired, kept the cab floor clean, adjusted the injector, lowered the tender water scoop when necessary, and observed some signals as well. There was no time really to sit down; the few seconds of grace between spells of work would be taken leaning on the cab side, head out of the window, to let the cooling wind refresh one for each new round and fill one's lungs with gulps of cold air.

One of the peculiarities of runs from London to Crewe was the passage of Linslade Tunnel, just north of Leighton Buzzard. This short single-track bore was renowned for the presence of a type of 'brick wall' atmospheric effect. The engine literally smashed its way through the narrow confines of the tunnel, fighting a compression of air with a clap like thunder. This compression caused the fire to dart back into the cab and to smother the crew with flames and smoke. Even with precautionary measures, such as closing the damper and putting the blower hard on, the fire would tend to blow back and the only thing one could do to protect oneself was to bury one's head in one's jacket, huddle in the corner of the cab and choke until the tunnel had been cleared. The smoke was augmented by nothing short of a minor dust storm during its brief passage. I know of no other tunnel which compared with the discomfort of Linslade; numerous drivers I fired for had been half choked or burned in the past, and all treated it with the utmost respect! some indeed swore that the supernatural lurked within it! By comparison Kilsby Tunnel, despite its terrors during construction —was much less troublesome; although much longer, it was double-track and its great shafts to the surface helped to keep it relatively exhaust-free. Indeed, it had no problems other than damp rails.

The run I am now going to describe was about the hardest one I ever had from Euston to Crewe. We had come south with Jubilee 4-6-0 No 45643, assisting Royal Scot No 46144 with the Perth–London sleeper due out of Crewe at 5.30am. The load was about 16 coaches, and due to

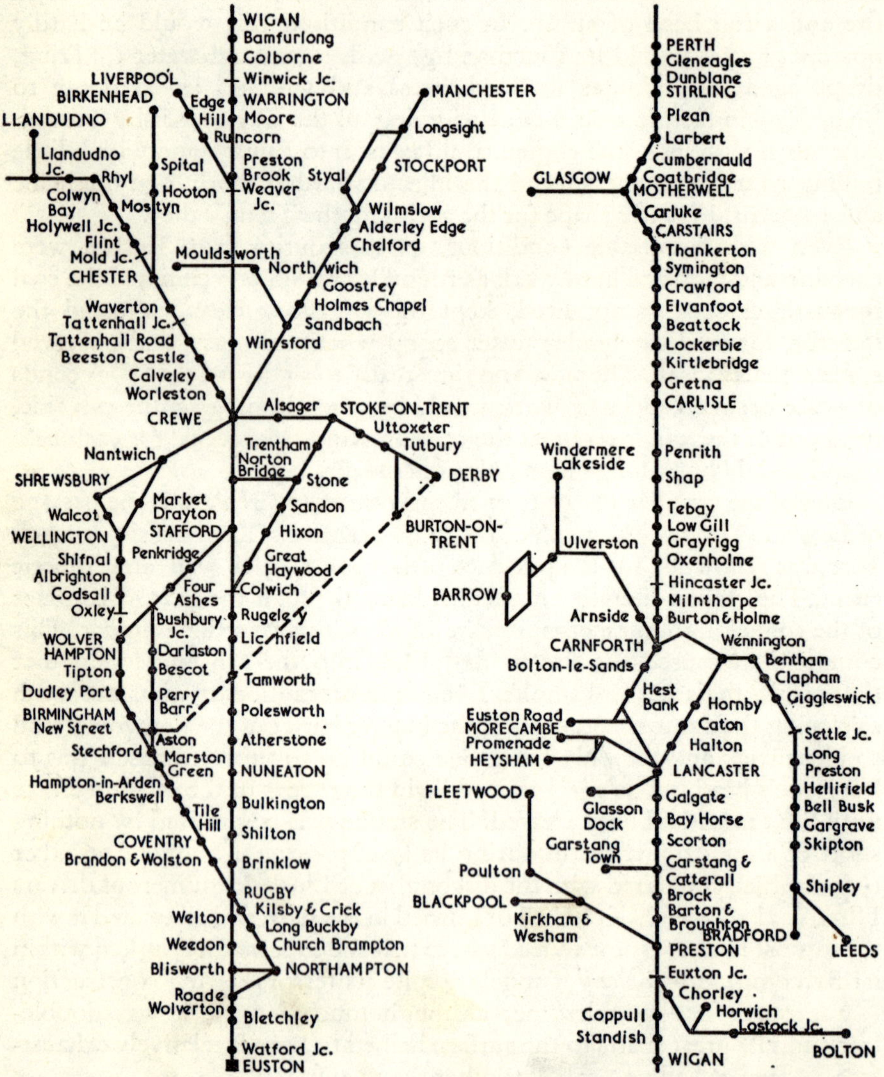

Diagrammatic Map indicating lines over which the author obtained firing experience.

out-of-course stops and shortage of steam the train had reached Crewe some 75min late. So we left Crewe at 6.48am and with stops at Nuneaton and Rugby made the run to Euston, arriving at about 10am. No 45643 was rough but otherwise seemed all right. It is deceptive, however, to try to estimate the individual work of either locomotive when double-heading, so I had to await the balance run that evening really to estimate No 45643's worth. Our return assignment was the 8.52pm to Holyhead, the relief 'Irish Mail'. The first part, with a Britannia 4–6–2 and 12 coaches, left at 8.45pm. We backed down to Euston to find waiting for us a 14-coach train of 457 tons tare, about 480 tons gross. This was a little more than I had bargained for and, I felt, more of a task for a Royal Scot. In typical style we left Euston without the fire built up as well as I liked but quite bright and, by rights, we should have been well burned through and hot by Willesden.

Alas, this was not to be! Not unnaturally, perhaps, we had dropped a couple of minutes by Willesden; then between Willesden and Hatch End the chimney succeeded in emulating all that is reputed of the LNWR locomotive in the past—a solid stream of hot sparks and cinders driven high into the sky amidst a constant pall of smoke. For some reason or other she would not produce enough steam, despite a dazzling white-hot fire which burned the seat of my overalls between each helping of coal. Worse still, the exhaust injector proved incapable of supplying all the needs of the boiler, and with the pressure at about 210lb the live steam one was required as well. I gave the fire a good pull through but found neither clinker nor unburned coal. The fire-irons were hardly stowed away when it was time to top up the tender tank over at Bushey troughs, by which time we ought to have been through Watford Junction.

The additional injector had put a doubtful expression on the 'clock' and I had no option but to shut it off and try and rally the fire somewhat. There seemed little doubt that this particular boiler was extended to the limit, but that limit was just not enough. My mate tried to console me a little by pointing to the reverser and indicating that we could whip her still more if I could produce any more steam. This had precisely the opposite effect on me and I had by now resigned myself to a rough trip, and rough it proved to be.

Nothing is more calculated to destroy the last few shreds of a fireman's hope than water bobbing in the bottom end of the gauge-glass, but by Tring this was where the water had dropped, and we had lost too much time to ease up downhill to Bletchley. Somewhat startled I noticed also that this particular Jubilee had a hell of an appetite, and that a considerable hole had been made in the tender coal supply, to such an extent, indeed, that I resorted to pulling it forward before Bletchley. This was the last straw! I had tried all I knew to make more steam and now realised that this was a battle I had lost at the start. It was a case of keeping going, nothing more. So I fired about eight shovelsful at a time and kept this up with monotonous regularity. The stream of fire from the chimney erupted with greater violence as I began to feed what presumably had come from the bottom of the Camden coal hopper. The small broken coal and dust was pouring out of the chimney in a brilliant stream.

The battle by now had become too much for one man and my mate had to have a go. Between us, and by sacrificing a further minute or two, we had managed to build up the water level somewhat and shut the injector off to regain boiler pressure. Things continued to be touch-and-go to Rugby and Kilsby Tunnel had to be threaded with steam still hard on, something unusual in itself. The Rugby stop, of some duration to allow for mail work, proved a godsend and we managed to depart with a full boiler, a reasonable head of steam and a really good fire. However, we were late and No 45643 had to be flogged continually in an effort to lose no further time. The coal supply had dwindled considerably and I spent some time in dragging it forward on the tender. My arms were becoming like lead weights and the roar from the front end was frightening. By Stafford I was 'all in'; the coal had receded to the very back of the tender and the fire began to loose depth, to the accompaniment of increasing showers of cinders. I was too tired by now to work the coal forward and to fire, so my mate, who fortunately was still able enough, fired her to Whitmore. Never had I been so thankful to see the approach to Crewe. I had not had such a mauling since the run on the boat train at Lancaster. So we reached Crewe at 12.28am, 18min late, on a schedule which included 12min recovery time. There were no medals for this night's effort. The coal supply had been depleted to such an extent that we had to tie the tender doors open to facilitate a more rapid approach to the 'mine'. On arrival we were relieved by a set of Chester men, all set for Holyhead. I did not hang about, but I can't help thinking that even if they had used the floorboards to supplement the coal supply, they would not have got as far as Rhyl, never mind Holyhead, with the amount of coal remaining on the tender.

This sort of run and others of a somewhat easier demand, highlighted the difficulty of work on the southern section of the main line, on which there were no steep grades to coast down and no stretches akin to the Warrington–Preston section, with its slacks which allow for boiler recovery. It was a road demanding hard continuous work, with little or no easing. Runs like that on No 45643, well loaded if not actually overloaded and with virtually no margin for erratic steaming or any other ailments, underlined the lack of adequate power for this line. Throughout the year, summer and winter alike, locomotives were being up-graded, often above

The unique rebuilt Scot 4–6–0 No 46170 *British Legion* *G. Wheeler*

Princess Royal 4–6–2 No 46027 *Princess Arthur of Connaught* **has its fire cleaned and is prepared for duty later in the evening at Camden m.p.d. in August 1961** *Colin P. Walker*

A Class 4 2–6–4T leaves Skipton on a local *Eric Treacy*

Princess Coronation 4–6–2 No 46232 *Duchess of Montrose* **climbs the 1 in 131 from Carlisle to Wreay with a Glasgow–Birmingham express in October 1961** *R. Leslie*

Footplate of Class 8P Pacific No 46226 *Duchess of Norfolk* *British Railways*

Footplate of BR Standard Class 4 4-6-0 No 75000 *British Railways*

Gretna Junction in August 1964: Britannia Pacific No 70049 on the Birmingham–Glasgow express *Derek Cross*

their limits, to make up for the shortage of Class 7 and Class 8 power. Power of the Class 6 standard was a dubious rating at the best of times, and perhaps better interpreted as 5-*plus* and no more (incidentally, the Patriots and Jubilees were formerly classified by the LMS as 5X). Lack of proper liaison between the locomotive department and the traffic department proper also helped to produce overloads like that behind No 45643.

Had our Jubilee been a little more on top of her job we might have done better, but in cases of doubt, as with the load in question, a Royal Scot should have been provided or, failing this, an assistant engine. Why the Britannia was not given two of our coaches I do not know, but having a bias against standard locomotives I had better not dwell on this matter. Another point highlighted by this run was the question of safety. My driver had his hands well and truly full in attempting to keep his train running, to humour a poor steamer and to help out with the shovel. Without an intimate knowledge of the road he might easily have missed a distant signal and thus caused a disaster. While the antics on No 45643 were not, fortunately, an everyday occurrence they were not uncommon and combined efforts with the shovel were often necessary if time as nearly as possible was to be kept.

Of the many duties undertaken on the Southern section which terminated at Rugby, one of mine on occasions usually had an un-rebuilt Patriot for motive power. The duty was a parcels train from Crewe to London, often loaded to considerable proportions, approaching 500 tons *plus*. The engines on this duty were all Willesden ones, and all had one failing—dirty boilers. Some of them primed with more than 'half a glass', and once on the climb to Whitmore we nearly stalled because of this. On one week's work on this job I had alternately a Patriot and a Jubilee, making quite an interesting comparison. Despite the boiler trouble the Patriot had a greater reserve and really took some punishment without undue loss of steam, whereas the Jubilee had somewhat less in hand. In all fairness, however, the Jubilee seemed always to be the quicker off the mark, while the old Patriots took a little time to get warmed up.

From the firing point of view the Patriots responded wonderfully and so smartly did they perform that we sometimes endeavoured to outpace trains on the adjacent fast line to Stafford, with some success. Like any other class, a bad engine could be a varmint, and I had a run with No 45511 that taxed me before we reached Rugby. Steam was produced only by much prodding with the fire-irons, the jet hard on and clouds and clouds of smoke. Part of No 45511's trouble, peculiar to many Fowler engines, lay in the badly-fitted smokebox door, which leaked much air, and combined with a large quantity of ash became extremely scorched with her exertions.

Much of the land adjoining the line from just north of Stafford down the Trent Valley line was subject to severe flooding and one could sometimes run for miles beside an artificial lake of enormous proportions. At one point we passed a small public-house sited in a particularly low-lying section, the 'Pretty Pigs'. On one occasion this was flooded to such a depth that the beer barrels (by repute) floated some distance away—alongside the line an enormous temptation to thirsty enginemen!

At both Tamworth and Lichfield large numbers of engine spotters congregated, very often upwards of 100, and no matter how hard one ran through these places the roars of pleasure or derision (depending on the particular engine) were every bit as good as from the average crowd at a football match. To encourage louder yells we would attempt to conceal the engine numbers, which would arouse screams of disapproval and much shaking of fists.

The Trent Valley was renowned for fog, and I had some very bad runs owing to this trouble. On one run with the 1.20am from Crewe to London and the 5.40pm from Glasgow, we took over the train at Crewe with Royal Scot No 46152 and departed some 12min late. The train was quite light, some 12 coaches and a horsebox (352 tons in all) and we made a great effort to regain time. After winning back several minutes we ran into fog and caught a 'distant' against us, rather late, just north of Tamworth. My mate gave an emergency application and we ground to an abrupt halt. On trying to release the brakes we could create no vacuum, and so had to test all the likely points of failure. I gradually made my way down the train, finding no fault until just at the end, when I was about to give up, I found that the vacuum pipe had jumped off the plug at the back of the horsebox. Probably the braking had been so severe that the pipe jerked off. By now our regained time had reverted to a 15min loss and the thick fog precluded any further recovery.

At Rugby we were relieved and worked our return on an 8F 2–8–0 with a semi-fitted freight, slogging slowly back to Crewe in some four hours. Rugby at this time was the bane of Crewe men. It became quite difficult to get past Rugby without being relieved; indeed, the number of spare men was so great that the chance of earning a fortune on a special through working to London was remote. Sometimes a bargain could be concluded with Control, especially when they were short of men. A set of men at Crewe, with perhaps five or six hours done, would be asked by Control whether they would like to man a certain job—a London turn for example. The cautious driver might play 'blind' and say that the job (to be relieved at Stafford or Rugby) was not worth the candle, and would hold out for London and home as passengers on the cushions. If Control was desperate enough, they might concede. So far, so good. During the run, however,

Control might find a spare set of men at Rugby and attempt to relieve, especially on a job which required a stop for examination. Here it depended on the driver. Some men were not prepared to be bullied, refused relief and carried on, while others, more timid, would concede victory to Control and settle for only half a pound instead of the pound that would be the reward for working through to London.

At some places where Control arranged relief—Carnforth was a good example—the signals would force one to a near stand in the station to permit a quick change-over, and almost immediately both 'boards' would pull off for 'right away'. Here skill and cunning played a part and a wily crew would crack right away to Carlisle and pretend that they had not seen any relief! Generally, however, this manœuvre was countered, and signals were held firmly against the engine until the relief crew acknowledged by whistle that the change had been made.

This subject of Control and enginemen could be debated at length. Considerable cunning was devised by both sides to further their particular ends. Train Control, when desperate for a set of men to work a special or cover some contingency, would promise the earth and just as easily exploit a set of men most unfairly. In the case of the down 'Midday Scott' Control were able to get their own back. This job often required a pilot in summer, even when hauled by a Duchess. Frequently this assisting engine would be a 2P 4–4–0. Now I am unable to give any good reason for this, especially when the train engine was a 4–6–2. Apart from providing a steady smoke screen for the driver of the train engine, the pilot rarely accomplished much else, and sometimes, as I will now tell, became a distinct liability.

No 46220 was the train engine on this occasion, and while I am not quite sure of the train load, I do not believe it was quite to the limit. However, our engine, No 40679, definitely was! To Carnforth all went well enough (as indeed it ought) for we had done no more than keep out of No 46220's way, but from hereon my mate attempted genuine assistance. With full regulator and an impressive roar we sailed through Carnforth, and onwards towards Oxenholme. The boiler, however, was not as anxious as the driver and a downward move in pressure became more than apparent. The only response from my mate was a few more turns on the wheel—in the wrong direction! Climbing from Oxenholme up Grayrigg bank, by Hay Fell the show was all but over, for we were down to 120lb of steam and with no water in sight. But the worst was yet to come. Some fellside demon had perversely arranged for an empty stock train to be slow in getting inside the loop at Grayrigg and we were brought to a stand. Vigorous 'poking' produced some billowing clouds of smoke and a little more steam, while a labouring injector coaxed an inch or so of water into the glass, albeit on a 1 in 106 grade! On restarting poor No 46220 had no option but to pull the Midday Scot and push No 40679 through Tebay and up to Shap Summit. All the time lost in this extra effort, however, was regained by a particularly lively descent to Carlisle, where we arrived 3min early.

Now 2P 4-4-0s were not very welcome at Carlisle, for their uselessness had penetrated to the powers-that-be there, and the latter were most anxious to ensure that whoever brought them in removed them after a suitable rest for all concerned. Though Carlisle Control staff had no compunction when it came to removing unwanted Crewe 2Ps they flatly refused to let the engines run home light. They had a much better idea; the owners of the 2P would have to book on at about 4.30am to get ready to assist the 6.10am 'all-stations' to Crewe! The train engine-crew on the job were relieved at Preston but the crew of the 2P were faced with 141 miles of travel and about 17 stops, to be completed in 6hr 10min, one of the few jobs I knew that made a driver's arm ache, for a change. Control justified this on the grounds that light engines tended to obstruct ordinary traffic and cause delay. But on her own No 40679 could have kept clear of anything else on the way, and raced like a hare back to Crewe in but a third of the time the 6.10 took.

A run to Glasgow as assistant engine on the Midday Scot with 'Black Stanier' 4-6-0 No 44685 proved a rather pleasant experience. The train engine was No 46228, and having behind us one of the best Pacifics, the job was no trouble at all. On the down 'Midday' thirsty crews were unable to get a drink in Glasgow as the pubs were closed by the time they booked off. The procedure, therefore, was to do a sprint at Carstairs to the refreshment-room to obtain the necessary bottles. On the run with No 44685 my mate got bottles for both ourselves and the train enginemen. On this occasion it was rather amusing as he dropped a bit of time *en route*, and No 46228 had got the train under way while he was still running down the platform. We detached at Polmadie and ran on to the shed, as the two engines coupled were not permitted to cross the Clyde bridge. Our return the following day with a relief to Birmingham was a great disappointment, our efforts to keep time being foiled by persistent signal checks to such an extent that we arrived in Crewe an hour late.

Coming south from Carlisle the long climb to Shap Summit made it a harder task than that in the opposite direction. I rarely did well until after Penrith, always finding it difficult to get my engines warmed up quickly enough. A run which caused me some initial trouble was with standard Class 5 4-6-0 No 73075 on a Glasgow-Liverpool job. We received her in Citadel Station in rather poor shape, with about half a glass of water and a blue fire. The tender had a bank of Polmadie 'muck' for fuel, and we had some difficulties to Penrith, our first stop. After Penrith matters improved considerably and I had the liveliest run down from Shap that I ever remember. Throughout the journey tender cupboards, lids and catches burst open and clanked or shook loose. She was very rough and the din and clatter were terrific. To some extent this noise was amplified by the metal cab floor. Non-standard engines had wooden floors which, although subject to greater wear than the metal ones, did to some extent deaden the volume of noise in the cab. In addition No 73075 had numerous small faults, including a defective speedometer. This was a pity because I feel sure that the speed we reached must have been spectacular. We were relieved at Preston and rode home 'passenger' to Crewe.

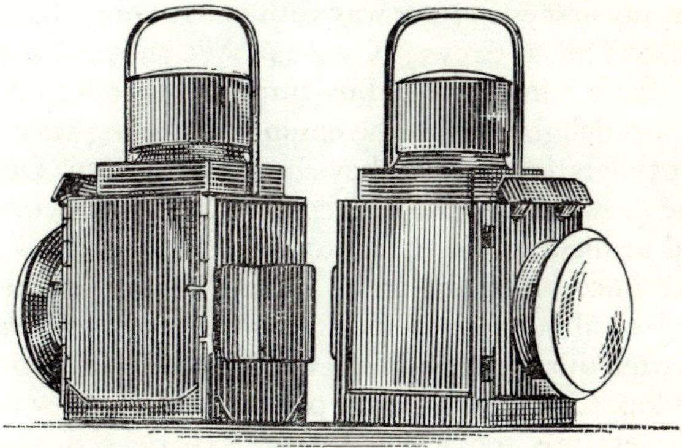

10

Firing a Duchess

Secretly I had looked forward to my first run with a Duchess, though I expected, nevertheless, to have little time to appreciate it. As things turned out, however, my first encounter was with one running 'light engine' from Liverpool Edge Hill to Crewe, No 46248. We should have followed the 7.5am 'slow' from Lime Street, but surprisingly were allowed away in front of it. I was delighted with the engine; the riding was superb and the acceleration exhilarating, just as they should have been. During the short run I learned how to operate the coal-pusher, and became reasonably accomplished at flicking the coal into the back corners and sides of the wide firebox. Once on to the main line at Weaver Junction we merely worked her up to about 70mph and shut off, letting her coast much of the way home. After this pleasant initial experience I sampled Duchesses on turns to London, Carlisle and Perth, chiefly north of Crewe.

A bad Duchess was something I never experienced, though on occasions I felt distinctly at sea firing them, and consequently things were not quite so good. To anyone not acquainted with working on locomotives it is difficult to convey the effects of handling these engines. Every time I worked on them I could not help feeling extremely impressed with their power. No other engine compared with them. Sometimes this was almost frightening and one's only defence 'against the blast'—a mere puny shovel—seemed most inadequate as one stood in a moment of indecision with a shovelful of coal poised in front of the firehole door, it was almost sucked off the shovel into the firebox!

Frankly, I never fired one of these engines often enough to take them for granted, and they always created in me an overwhelming impression of might and power, for which I seemed so poor a match. Consequently I took no chances with them, and was always liberal with coal, keeping a well-filled box, and never allowing the blast to pull all the 'back-crust' away. A round of coal on a Duchess for me would usually be 20 or so shovelsful, and more if necessary. There was never any need to break up coal for this—not as long as it would enter the firehole—for when working hard they would consume anything, including numerous pairs of overall trousers.

Preparing the fire on a Duchess required a great deal of effort, as one usually filled right up to the firehole and some two-thirds of the way down the grate—something like a ton or more of coal. Large lump coal was ideal, and when such was available one would build the fire up by hand, allowing plenty of air space to produce an ideal 'loose' fire. Apart from the ease of ordinary firing over the first miles, the large quantity of fuel already available in the firebox allowed for extra coal to be dropped into the tender—an important point to ensure a sufficient supply with the Duchess on long runs. The Perth run was conducted in this way, a massive fire being carefully built up followed by a final topping-up of the tender and often, if the size was right, a few hundredweights of lumps in the cab for the first round. The tender was not topped up in the ordinary way, but the process took some time; the fireman stacked the larger lumps on and along the tender sides to allow of as great an amount of coal as possible to be packed in the centre, often higher than the cab roof.

On estimate, I doubt whether any Duchess on the Perth run left Crewe with much less than 12 tons of coal and probably more—10-ton tender capacity or not! But why the desire for so much extra coal? Quite simply it was a question of reserve. With 292 miles of running ahead, including the steep climbs to three summits, any kind of weather conditions could prevail, and the added resistance of a heavy side wind, often near gale force, could absorb considerably more fuel than in favourable conditions. Coal of a grade poorer than normal would require a larger amount to produce the necessary steam, and bitter experience of clearing up the last few hundredweights when climbing through Dunblane or, worse still, even before that, had taught drivers to ensure a maximum capacity. The big fire on a northbound Duchess, if carefully controlled, could certainly take me to Preston, and I have heard of a Duchess going considerably farther with very little attention. The regular Perth firemen could, I believe, take an engine all the way with no more than about 8 to 12 firings, though each firing would consist of a very large number of full shovels.

Needless to say, the Perth duties were quite the toughest runs at Crewe and, among the younger hands, were considered almost as an approach to heaven. One's status was heightened considerably if one had been to Perth. Not all firemen, however, felt quite the same way about this or, at least, some appeared not to, for more than a few failed for one reason or another to turn up for these duties. Spare men could feel reasonably sure that they had no more than a 50–50 chance of sampling the job, and it was with no little surprise that one day I found myself booked for the 10.34pm from Crewe to Perth. I had in fact booked off duty the same morning at

7.50 with no definite job to follow and I was just marked to come in as an 8pm spare. I had been to bed and got up at about six o'clock to go to my local for a 'session'. These sessions usually accounted for six or seven pints and I was through my fifth when someone came round from my lodgings to impart the glad tidings. This meant arriving at work at about 9pm. The shock—for shock it was—quickly sobered me, and I hastily gathered together some supplies—drinking water, cigarettes, food, brush and all the other oddments I faithfully carried around, but never needed such as split pins, corks, gauge-glass and the like.

I arrived quite early and proceeded to prepare my fire, clean up the cab and oil all those points that preparers never seemed to touch—injector, gauge-glass cocks, dampers, and so on. The ritual of the tender filling and trimming was gone through and I 'brewed up' and sat down, feet up, to watch the flames lick slowly through the deep bank of cobbles carefully heaped under the firehole door. With about 220lb 'on the clock' and half a glass of water, we backed into the station and on to our train of 11 coaches with two horseboxes, about 418 tons in all. I felt both proud and nervous. The engine, No 46249, was only the third Duchess that I had fired and the distance to be covered seemed enormous. The coal on the tender assumed vast proportions and I began to think of all the things that could go wrong. At 10.25 I coupled up and changed the lamps, put the injector on to top up the boiler and soon we were away. I kicked the flap up and lit a cigarette to get a grip on the situation.

Gradually we picked up speed and left Crewe far behind. No great effort was needed, but there was just a steady 'clickety-click' as we gained speed on the favourable grades through Winsford, Hartford, Acton Bridge and on through Weaver Junction and towards Moore troughs where I topped up the tender. Through Warrington we sped (it seemed to be permanently daylight here), then up to Golborne and on towards Wigan. From there the climb through Boars Head caused me to pick up the shovel for the first time and I carefully topped up the back and sides of the firebox and sat down again as we rolled cautiously down to Preston.

By now I had resigned myself to anything that might happen. Somehow I was to fire on this engine till nearly 6 in the morning and somehow we would get there. And get there we did and, furthermore, without the fuss and bother that I had anticipated. True, we were not exactly overloaded, but No 46249 simply purred along and the whole job seemed to go like clockwork. We tore through Lancaster—not without my reflecting on its past significance—and on to Carnforth and then came the start of the climb to Shap, I should say 'climb', but we hardly felt it. The final climb at 1 in 75 from Tebay to the summit that night was particularly pleasing to me—plenty of steam, a nice crisp beat, the cold, clean fellside air cutting into my face, and the feeling of pleasure derived from an engine so comfortably on top of its job.

Although all was well I kept pushing the cobbles into the box, not daring to let the fire get too low. The descent to Penrith was taken quite steadily and we arrived at Carlisle with a minute or so in hand. On restarting our journey north things were uneventful until after Floriston, where the troughs were out of order, so that we had to pull up in Beattock Station for a drink. Here the night air was cooler than I had imagined, for the ladder at the back of the tender was slippery with frost, and the tank lid had to be battered with the coal pick before I could open it. The leather water bag also was stiff with frost and had to be 'beaten' into the tank.

Having filled up we restarted, and without any slips or steam trouble reached the summit. Here the exhaust injector decided to play up and I had to work the live steam injector till I could humour the exhaust once more. At Motherwell we topped up the tank again, and enjoyed a cup of tea provided by the guard, a regular feature of the turn. Little of note occurred during the running through Larbert and Stirling, but an impressive effort was made up the 1 in 100–88 past Dunblane to Kinbuck and on to Gleneagles, from here 'feet up' was the order of the day and we coasted down to Perth. After uncoupling we ran to the shed and booked off duty at 5.45. I felt wide awake and not in the least tired.

The same evening we booked on duty at 7.45 pm for the 8.15 sleeper to Crewe, with twelve coaches, given as 389 tons and No 46249 again. Weather conditions had now changed considerably and a strong wind, which developed into gale force, was to play havoc with our return. We had a supply of rather small Scotch coal, a reasonable fire, but no opportunity to top up our tender as customary at Crewe, and so had to be careful. The coal had some heat in it for we blew off steam steadily up to Gleneagles, but the higher we climbed the more severe the wind became, and so strong eventually that I was forced to close my side window, an unprecedented happening so far as I was concerned. Racing down from Kinbuck through Dunblane my water bottle, which I thought I had stowed safely on the tender near the coal-pusher lever, vanished without trace. To this day I believe it just blew out of the cab, for no sign of broken glass was found. The high wind persisted all the way to Preston, by which time I was in great trouble with coal. Between here and Warrington I was dragging the few remaining hundredweights to the tender fall-plate, as we had too little for the pusher to act on. By Warrington the fire was breaking (myself physically and the tender practically) and we scraped into Crewe with about 160lb of steam and only a few bucketsful of slack left.

For me it had been a tremendous experience and in many ways a climax to my footplate career. While of short duration only, this had had its moments of despair, of times when I nearly packed the job in altogether, and the cruel period at Burton when I felt lost in a hopeless situation, reduced at times to working on engines of minute dimensions and perpetually shunting. Never in my wildest dreams had I envisaged working to Perth, but I had accomplished it, and done quite well. There were no illusions, however, and I very much doubted whether I could stand the pace of such a duty regularly. One had to be really physically fit, to eat well and sleep well, to do that sort of firing; it was, in fact, a man-size job, entailing as it did heaving something like 65lb of coal per mile for 300 miles in some seven hours. This was 'graft' with a vengeance! It is worth noting, in connection with the Perth duties, that Perth men themselves had apparently declined to balance the job by working south to Crewe. On reflection, I didn't altogether blame them.

Though I mastered the wide grate of the Duchesses, I never quite managed those of the Britannia Pacifics. I remember one double trip to London with, on the outward leg, Duchess No 46225—a splendid engine which simply made light of the job. On the return we had Britannia No 70048 to Crewe via Northampton and Birmingham. It was as well that we had some stops to make, for they enabled me to regain pressure and soak my hands in oil to cool the burns, for I disliked firing with gloves on. From time to time I had tried them, but on one occasion I let the shovel fall into the firebox through the lack of touch. Furthermore, they were just another item which all too soon became worn or mislaid, and until this run with the Britannia I had little or no use for them.

Almost my last main-line run at Crewe turned out to be rather eventful. The date was November 11, Remembrance Day, and a remembrance it will for ever remain. I booked on duty at 8.55 for the 9.10am London parcels, which we were to work as far as Rugby, with Class 5 No 45282 and a 341-ton load. It was a crisp morning, the sort of day with a cold snap just sufficient to keep one on the move, alert and on top of the job. I liked cold weather on the engines; I could even swear that a locomotive steamed better in frosty weather than in muggy, close conditions. The fire always seemed bright and full of life and eager to burn, which was not always so on hot summer days or on damp, listless ones. But to return to the point. We steamed slowly out of Crewe, past Basford Sidings, where Patriot 4-6-0 No 45500, polished and resplendent and decorated with poppies, was standing by, presumably also bound for Rugby. The run proceeded uneventfully up the bank to Whitmore, after which we gained speed down to Stafford.

Somewhere on this section a most unusual thing happened—a large swan flew across the line just in front of our engine, so close indeed that had this been a few seconds later, we should have hit it. Now I am a very superstitious person, careful to avoid walking under ladders, fearing the thirteenth of the month, lone magpies and other similar portents. To me this was definitely a sign, but of what I had no idea. However, I let the matter pass and we duly arrived at Rugby, where straight away we relieved the crew on a Willesden–Crewe fitted freight, engine No 45296, with a load of 48 wagons. On the way north we were stopped at Shilton box and warned of sheep on the line. After this check we thumped our train to Stafford in good time, only to be put round the back road and held there for a while. This upset my mate somewhat and we did not work quite so hard up to Whitmore. We approached Basford Hall on the slow line at reduced speed, to allow the Broad Street to Glasgow meat train into the yard first. By now the weather had changed and it was pitch dark and raining heavily.

We had been standing at the gantry protecting the entrance to Basford Yards for some time when a signal dropped and we released the brakes. At almost precisely the same moment another Class 5, on a fitted freight bound for London and working heavily came roaring past us. Suddenly, without any warning, there was a terrific crash and I found myself lying on the cab floor, dazed and bruised. My mate appeared to be knocked out 'cold' over the reverser. He came to, however, and rather dizzily we picked ourselves up. I looked back but could see nothing. Climbing off the engine I ran back and came to a gigantic heap of wrecked wagons, mixed up with an overturned locomotive. I immediately thought of our guard; it seemed impossible that he could have survived, for his brake-van was no more than a heap of matchwood. This made me feel sick inside and I started to shake all over. A bump about the size of an egg had appeared on the back of my head.

Suddenly it dawned on me that here was I standing by with all four main lines blocked. For a second I froze, then raced back to the engine and, accompanied by my mate, hurried to the nearby signalbox to report. The signalman was quite unaware what had happened but immediately put all signals at danger. This done, we returned to the rear of the train and, lo and behold, who should be there poking about in the wreckage but our guard! Apparently he had been standing on his van veranda and, seeing the other train approaching at speed he had jumped off. By so doing he had saved his life.

Three trains were involved. One had collided with the rear of our train, the wreckage fouling the up slow line and derailed the London-bound freight, the engine of which was lying on its side. Returning to our engine we found water pouring down the tubeplate from numerous tubes, which had been loosened by the shock of the collision. Our information to the signalman had just been in time, for a down Liverpool express was working up the bank towards Whitmore and was stopped in time.

That night I felt thankful to book off and felt that I now understood what the omen of the swan meant. Fortunately no one was seriously injured in the smash, but to me at least, it did point out the necessity for constant vigilance on the footplate. The line we were standing on at Basford was worked by permissive block, and trains would often build up, nose to tail, on this section. The driver of the parcels train in our rear had under-estimated his speed and was unable to pull up in time. I never did like this method of signalling, for it placed too much reliance on drivers in estimating their speed. However, I was fortunate in coming through this experience with so little personal damage.

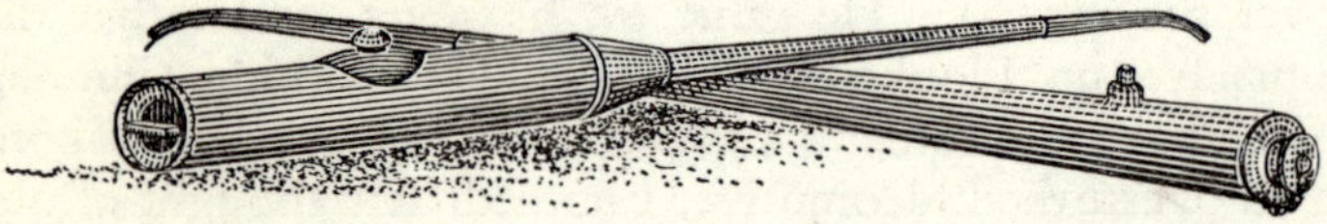

11

A Footplate Miscellany

The word dismal fittingly described Stockport and might equally well be applied to my first run to that place. I did not find the combination of a Caprotti-fitted 'Black 5' and 43 loaded wagons a happy one. The train itself was a through Bescot–Adswood sidings fitted freight and No 44751 made heavy weather of it, notwithstanding an ample supply of steam. We left Crewe in a shroud of it, originating from somewhere up in front, and even before we had climbed out of the freight cutting the exhaust injector packed up. Once on the Manchester road progress was decidedly laboured, for despite an indicated cut-off of 35 per cent, full regulator and boiler pressure steady at 210lb the steam just trickled out of the chimney in sickly 'chuffs'. Progress was poor enough to have us turned into the loop at Chelford until two passenger trains had passed. Once again we were brought to rest at Wilmslow and were informed by the signalman that we had overshot the signal; the track circuiting must have been at fault for we were two wagon-lengths from it. Regrettably this run was all too typical of my experiences with Caprotti class 5s; I had found them equally lethargic when I was at Lancaster, particularly when hauling empties up the grade to Clapham.

One of my first duties on a LNW 0–8–0, No 49417, was in conditions similar to those prevailing on the 4F during trip duties from North Staffs siding to Basford Hall. The job was the 8.45 p.m. to Stoke, and we set off during a little blizzard. Our storm sheet tied from cab to tender acted more like a sail and whipped and cracked in the wind. We put off part of our train at Etruria and the remainder at Cockshute siding, Stoke, where we turned and proceeded tender first to Sideaway siding, about a mile down the line from Stoke, ostensibly to pick up a run of coal. On arrival at this aptly-named haven we found the points into the sidings were jammed, and so were we, for the best part of an hour. The night seemed to get colder and colder and still the snow fell. Eventually it was decided to abandon hope and return to Stoke. Here the powers-that-be placed us in the most exposed position possible, Glebe Street, where, elevated sufficiently to secure the full force of wind and snow, we sat and shivered. LNW 0–8–0s had virtually no cab at all and this, coupled with a great gap between engine and tender, succeeded in all but freezing us to death. In an endeavour to keep warm, I wedged myself in the narrow corner of my cab, exposing my back to the extremely hot metal of the firebox back-plate, and so, twisting and turning, alternately froze and fried back and front for well over an hour. Finally we were released and allowed to run home light engine to Crewe.

On another occasion with No 49417, this time on a Shrewsbury–Crewe freight, things—initially at least—seemed perfect. We had a tender full of Welsh coal, on which she steamed beautifully—so well, indeed, that I had great difficulty in preventing the safety-valves from blowing off. My luck did not hold out, however, and the run culminated in a rather sad event. All went as per the text-book until we topped the rise over the Shropshire Union Canal, approaching Nantwich, where we were checked for a WR train off the Market Drayton line. To keep our engine quiet I had to keep one injector on all the time, even through the station. There are two level crossings at Nantwich and when nearing the second, at the Crewe end, we opened the regulator up in order to get under way again. With a roar she blasted a torrent of filthy, sooty water in a seemingly endless stream high into the air. Unfortunately the crossing-keeper's wife was just hanging out her washing, and I regret to say that that day she had no alternative but to start all over again. We remained semi-hydraulic for some time, and, in fact, still had plenty of water in the boiler when passing Gresty shed.

A not-so-pleasant run on the Shrewsbury line involved ex-WD 2–8–0. No 90385 on a through York–Salop train of iron bars and slabs. On relieving the crew I found a beautiful blue-black fire, inches deep with clinker, and the coal right at the back of the tender. Half an hour was spent in poking the fire into some sort of order and dragging a supply of coal forward. Despite these noble efforts, much smoke and a lot of heavy exhaust found us with 150lb of steam at the top of Wrenbury Bank and no more than 1½in of water in the glass. This indifferent response continued to Shrewsbury, where we booked the engine for not steaming. A point of interest was a part-bucket of sand, probably used by the previous crew in an endeavour to clean the tubes.

My experiences generally with the WD engines were very mixed. As long as one accepted the fact that they were a makeshift effort, one could understand why they usually had some ailment or other. They were often indescribably rough with a pronounced side-to-side waggle. The oft-reported tender 'thump-thump-thumping' against the engine seemed common to all of them. The lubrication, mainly sight-feed of one sort or another, seemed very neglected and seldom functioned properly. A peculiarity, I often found, was the difficulty of being certain of the level of water in the boiler. On several occasions I had glasses apparently full one minute and almost empty the next. The steam brake on these engines was not as strong as it should have been and in general they seemed very much neglected. Compared with the Standard 8F or GW 28XX they were very poor tools, and I certainly did not envy anyone who had charge of them.

The Shrewsbury line had several other special memories for me, including work with the Engineer's Saloon and running-in ex-works engines on 'trials'. Of the former, on the only occasion on which I fired we had a splendid day ambling along the line between Whitchurch and Hadnall. About lunch-time we took to a siding to allow the occupants of the saloon to enjoy their lunch. Somewhat surprisingly the cook presented us both with a lovely salad, sweet and a cup of tea. I had worked the Engineer's Saloon often at Lancaster, but had never been offered so much as a crust. Needless to say, I had a high regard for the Crewe District Engineer!

To get booked for perhaps a week's work on 'trials' was a highly regarded prize. Engines fresh from the works were sent to the South Shed and run in, either singly or coupled, up and down the Shrewsbury line, usually as far as Yorton or Hadnell, then back to Whitchurch, where they were turned and stood over pits for inspection. This was undertaken mainly by a qualified examiner, Mr Woods. He had had the honour of accompanying No 6100 *Royal Scot* to America as a fitter, and certainly knew all the trouble spots that newly repaired engines were likely to possess. He was a very pleasant man and much respected by all the drivers on 'trials'. Inspection usually took an hour or so, and then we all had lunch. The somewhat congested state of the line made it difficult to get engines back to Crewe quickly, and we usually had quite a wait at Whitchurch.

Card games were therefore the order of the day on this job; the most comfortable engine would be selected, while those participating would bring buckets and shovels to sit on and a flat box lid (kept at Whitchurch) for the cards to be dealt on. Regretfully I was never very successful, and a week on 'trials' could prove rather expensive!

The work required on the engines going on trial was mainly that of preparation. All the various oil-boxes, motion and fittings required a vast amount of oil, and it was surprising just how much an empty big end on, say, a Royal Scot, could absorb. More often than not extra supplies of oil were required to complete the oiling of a big engine. One of the worst features of preparation was the question of the sandboxes. On engines fresh from works these were nearly always empty and one humped literally hundredweights of the stuff up and down engines until one's arms felt as though they would drop off. There must certainly be a lot in favour of the American principle of overhead sanding and pipe delivery.

Everything on a new engine was stiff. The reverser, for instance, often required both men to turn it, and needed flooding with oil to get it to operate anything like freely. The injectors were stiff, and sometimes their water regulators would only budge with assistance from the coal hammer. Dampers were another problem, and the rods, arms, pins and lever connections required plenty of oil and sometimes more persuasive measures to make them operate. Brakes tended to stick, and general weight distribution sometimes left a lot to be desired, necessitating adjustment of spring-loading before returning to the main line. Mechanical lubricators often required attention and adjustment to make them supply a flow of oil; sometimes they didn't feed at all. Gauge-glass shut-off cocks, tender water-cocks, blower-valves, tender sprinklers, slaking pipes and, above all, cylinder taps, tended to stick and the latter frequently did stick on trial engines, requiring considerable humouring before they would close properly.

The reverser, however, was usually the most troublesome piece of equipment on a newly-repaired engine. Many of the trial drivers were quite old men, who often strained themselves while attempting to operate a reverser. No matter how bad an LMS reverser might be, the standard version was usually very much worse, and on several occasions I fired for drivers who just could not turn them at all. In particular I remember how the reverser on a newly shopped Britannia, No 70004, almost beat me and provided a very strenuous day indeed. Regulators could also be bad, and, again, those of standard types were the worst. Much of this kind of trouble could undoubtedly have been cured by suitable attention in the works, but works schedules were so tight that delays in getting an engine back into service had to be answered for, with the result that the poor engine-driver on the trials would suffer.

The fires in trial engines had usually been lit for at least 24 hours and were sometimes very slow in making steam. On one trip which I remember, we were the middle engine of three, and had so little steam that reversing was our only real effort. During the run out and back to Whitchurch we cooked our lunch on the shovel—kippers and ham and eggs if I remember correctly.

Before finally leaving the Salop line, some mention of Shrewsbury shed would perhaps not be amiss. Although at one time this was technically a joint LMSR–GWR shed, to me it smacked more strongly of the latter, particularly as regards its footplate staff, who were decidedly GWR in outlook and character. Crewe men quite frequently went on shed here for an hour or so before taking a return working, and to sit in the mess-room was an education in itself, with the strongly conflicting accents of men from South Wales, London and the West Country vying with one another as to who could tell the biggest yarns. It should, of course, be made clear here that WR men transferred more freely and regularly than LMR men, hence the mixed accents.

The great point about Shrewsbury shed was the generally clean state of the locomotives. More often than not our engine would be a filthy South Shed one, uncleaned and grey-black, with probably only the number and the tender *motif* discernible. Just as often, and by way of contrast, one of the Shrewsbury pride and joys—an absolutely gleaming Castle 4-6-0 in beautiful green and brass—would be near by. Envy was not the word! I would have given a week's wages to be fireman on such an obviously pampered beast. Several cleaners were usually at work, putting final touches to the brasswork, name and number plates. The turn-out of their engines was marvellous. Castles, of course, were smart by any standard, and an LMR engine had to be really worked on to approach this standard; I should add, however, that Crewe North Shed did turn out some very clean express types, especially Duchesses and Royal Scots. For example, the Duchess for the Perth runs was usually turned out in near-immaculate condition but often returned looking as though it had not been touched for weeks. I had deep sympathy for the cleaners whose efforts were often so ruined after no more than twenty-four hours on the road.

To return to Shrewsbury, we had one turn which brought us on to that shed at about 6am, and frequently no fewer than three of the magnificent green and brass Western beauties were there on parade, surrounded by an army of attendants. Beside such a trio our own scruffy machine was indeed a disgrace; and not only Shrewsbury's Castles but most of the other engines there had obviously received attention. Even engines stored for months had been rubbed over. In another sense, this was a bad sign, for it usually indicated a large number of cleaners, a slow-promotion shed, and, consequently, much discipline. If engines had to be cleaned, I preferred to see it done with good facilities, plenty of the right type of cleaning materials, cloths and so on, and done regularly enough to ensure that the task was capable of producing some attractive results, rather than the all-too-often appearance of engines caked with filth and uncleaned for weeks which too often were the engine cleaner's lot.

In this book I have separated, to a certain extent, the Crewe shunting, freight and passenger workings. In actual fact I undertook the duties, as it were, simultaneously. While this provided excellent experience, it was not easy to accustom oneself to the differing approaches required by the intermittent variety of such duties. To be confined to runs of little more than 70 miles a day for weeks on end, and then to revert to working two or three times this mileage, was as difficult to conform to as was the variation in the hours that one was called for duty.

A short run with more than its fair share of excitement was the 2.4am newspaper train to Manchester, loaded usually to one or two vans, generally powered by a Royal Scot 4-6-0 or a Britannia 4-6-2. These runs with the newspapers must have been some of the fastest jobs I ever worked on, the pace from Crewe to London Road Station being positively electric!—a shocking phrase, I agree, but the most appropriate that I can think of. I often regret that I never timed our running on this turn for I am sure that some really exceptional timings were achieved.

Initial work in preparation for the electrification of the Manchester line created numerous ballast and similar workings connected with the blowing up of bridges, digging holes for pylons and allied work. Sometimes, when relieving other men on these turns, a BR bus was provided to take us to whatever remote part of the line the engine happened to be visiting. Mention of this line reminds me also of the occasion on which we went 'on safari' at Stockport. We had been relieved at Edgeley by a set of men who were to work our train on to Leeds and, as was usual, proceeded to the rest cabin at the end of the engine shed yard to have some rest until our balance working arrived. We entered the cabin to find another engine crew already installed—not perhaps unusual in itself. However, the fireman was lying down on a bench, poker in hand, raised over a small hole in the floor. It transpired that the cabin was infested with rats and he had already killed three before we arrived. This crew soon left to relieve another train, and I continued the good work, baiting the hole with pieces of bread and hitting the intruders every time they appeared. The grand total was some six or more young rats. While the catch had been proceeding, my mate remained almost hypnotised, and I noticed that what he saw had removed his urge to do justice to his lunch tin. On arrival back at Crewe we made out a most indignant report as to the state of this particular cabin and that was the last I heard of rats in that particular place.

Then there were some happenings on the Birmingham road. Once we relieved a train from Liverpool at Crewe and I noticed that the engine was rather low in both steam and water. The Edge Hill fireman said nothing but his sheepish expression should have conveyed a note of warning. On the engine and riding with us was a driver wanting to refresh his memory of the line in the Birmingham area. On our departure this kind soul volunteered to fire the engine to Stafford. He picked up the shovel and put on a good round of coal, allowing the engine to warm up through Betley Road and on to Madeley. However, things just did not go as planned and we steadily lost steam, falling to about 160lb pressure at Whitmore, but I decided to leave matters in the 'passenger's' hands. I had not invited him to fire the engine, and I was not really sure what ailed No 45410. Now, observing the decline on the 'clock', the visitor stripped his coat off and, wielding a fire-iron, proceeded to give the fire a really good pull through. Steam pressure rallied somewhat but not greatly so, and only by dint of much hammering did we keep time to Wolverhampton.

The return run on the same engine and with the fire cleaned a little, was somewhat better, but something else was troubling No 45410 and she was not a very good steamer. I have a particular reason for mentioning this run. I thoroughly disliked other people firing my engines as I often found that my methods of firing did not take kindly to any variants by a strange hand. In this instance I had not touched the fire but the principle still held good. Only when I was in great difficulty or feeling worn out would I hand over the shovel and, even then, reluctantly. Some drivers fired very well and could swing a shovel with the greatest of ease. Some had a passion for the shovel and swung it at the first opportunity. Others, and I fear there were quite a number of them, had completely forgotten how to fire—perhaps they had never even known how to. They would shoot vast quantities of coal just wherever it happened to fall and the results did not seem to worry them unduly. Some just could not fire to save their lives and would straighten up, puffing and panting, after about ten shots and pronounce the coal to be much heavier than it had been in their day.

On another run to Birmingham we had a pilotman, and he succeeded in distracting my mate just as we were approaching a speed limit, which we covered at about twice the specified rate. The speed board was located close by a signalbox at Bescot, and the crashes as we hit various points and crossings were really frightening. The balance job was with No 44692 on a special to Holyhead (which we had to work as far as Crewe). I had a passed fireman as driver and we must surely have broken the record back to Crewe that night. Our coal was small and streams of red hot cinders poured out in an endless shower all the way to Penkridge. At this point we had got sufficient momentum to take us to Stafford, where we opened out again in the same style, to top Whitmore in under 'even time'. With the same driver we had once thrashed a 'Crab' on a Birmingham express in the same way. On this occasion a cob of coal fell from the tender and unfortunately it hit the track, rebounded and broke a carriage window. Some time was lost at Stafford while a 'court of inquiry' was held. We regained some five minutes to Wolverhampton, but only by the boiler beating both injectors.

Apart from the large number of regular Crewe duties there were (particularly during the summer months) a great many special passenger jobs of one sort or another. Many excursions from the Birmingham and Stoke areas, bound for the North Wales coast, were remanned at Crewe and I had some extremely pleasant days out at the seaside at Rhyl, Llandudno and Blackpool. On one occasion we went as passengers to Blackpool, to work a return special of Southern stock bound for Southampton and Weymouth. Two amusing incidents with this job are worth recording. In the first instance our engine, No 73034, was 'lost' for a time, and when we did eventually find it the guard of the train came up to the engine to remind us that we were booked to take water at Basingstoke and other mysterious places, to which even Crewe men were unlikely ever to work. We tactfully pointed out that we should only be going as far as Crewe and he, somewhat crestfallen, returned to the train. During the mysterious absence of No 73034 her fire had been allowed to burn very low, and with the hard Yorkshire coal (with which Blackpool seemed usually blessed) we had not a great deal of steam until we passed Preston.

Crewe often remanned specials to and from big sporting events in London. The Rugby League Cup usually provided a spate of extra trains. I worked a number of these and on one occasion manned No 45073, which was earmarked as stand-by in Crewe Station, in case any of the Rugby special train engines might be ailing in any way. We took up our position about 1am, after about an hour of dutiful preparedness and I fell fast asleep until dawn, when I awoke feeling bitterly cold and with the fire almost out. If any special had been lethargic enough to be crawling into Crewe at this moment, requesting aid, they would have been in for a bit of a shock. It took me the best part of half an hour to pull the fire round and make steam enough to return to the shed!

In previous references to the Stoke line I mentioned the secondary nature of much of the work done over it. It had another unpleasant aspect—inordinate delays. Lost time on the run on the ex-LNW 0–8–0 to Sideaway was no doubt excusable on account of the snow. More often than not, however, little or no excuse was required to detain light engines. I have notes in my Crewe diary of a number of occasions when we took as long as four hours to return from Stoke to Crewe with a light engine, while from two or three hours was quite common. In fact, one might fairly say that it usually took longer to get out of the 'Pots' than to get in! On one of the few times when I worked through to Derby we had No 78030 and six coaches in place of the normal diesel multiple-unit set. To say that we did surprisingly well would be an understatement. We were badly checked at Normacot and I remember that the fire fairly leapt out of the chimney as we blasted through the tunnel on the 1 in 100 grade. She was a fine little runner, and we did 60mph and a little over on several stretches. At Derby we had a 'pint' and then returned light engine. On another run to Derby we had No 44180 on a Garston–Nottingham banana special. We quite expected relief at Stoke but none was forthcoming, though the guard was relieved there, and his relief in turn at Uttoxeter. Eventually we arrived in Derby too late to catch the last train back to Crewe. Any visions

I might have had of hours of overtime were dashed by the cunning of Control, who sent us home by the 12.17am to Birmingham, and from there with the 1.45am parcels to Crewe.

Perhaps the most deceptive feature of engine working was the question of speed. Apart from the Standards and the Pacifics, few LM engines had speedometers and speed estimation was consequently more guesswork than anything else. Speed restrictions up to 30 mph were usually properly adhered to, but above this speed I am not so sure. I had several very alarming experiences on sections of track with speed restrictions of 40 to 50mph or so; as recorded elsewhere, we all but came off the road at Bescot on one occasion because of excessive speed. When it was necessary and permissible to reach anything out of the ordinary in the way of speed, one needed favourable conditions, not the least of these being a keen driver—and the younger ones seemed more likely to seek the spectacular than the older men. Even when working on engines fitted with speedometers one could not be certain that they gave an accurate reading, they could err by as much as 10mph.

One night on the down 'Northern Irishman' with No 46250 we had a really clear road and were thus encouraged to 'let her roll'. Down Shap the speedometer was past the 100 mark near Eden Valley Junction. It is probable that we were not doing more than 90mph though we were certainly erring on the excess side, and had to correct the speed severely for the speed restriction through Penrith. This run and several others which approached the three-figure mark were with a Crewe driver, one Joe Rider, who had a reputation for not hanging about when given the road. I remember also a run back from Glasgow with Joe when we were checked all the way south, arriving at Crewe over an hour late. I never have seen a driver so fed up. Our engine, No 44685, was in first-class order and only wanted a clear road to really show her paces. It was not to be, however, and having endured the checks to Carnforth we lost interest after that and just ambled on to Crewe.

Unlike Lancaster, where I knew all the staff, I rarely got to know any drivers well at Crewe; with almost a different one every day this was only to be expected. There were some outstanding characters, of course, but generally speaking they were an easy-going crowd, not given to making much of their job and casual to a degree that surprised me; moreover, they were fully aware that engines perform better with a team rather than with a pair of individuals at the controls. When physically able they often insisted on helping their firemen, either working the scoop on the troughs, pulling coal forward, or firing a few rounds; they would use every possible means to make the fireman's work easier by easing the regulator or shutting off steam altogether in favourable conditions. Some of the younger drivers were extremely keen, possessed of a wide road knowledge, ever anxious to handle the top jobs, full of confidence and always ready to give encouragement to their firemen. They must have been a good crowd because I was not the easiest of people to get on with; nevertheless, I only fell out with one driver at Crewe—a shunt driver—under circumstances already mentioned. One other driver (I never did find out who he was) put me in a spot at one of my Crewe lodgings. I made some critical remarks about my sandwiches one day, and my comments were passed back to my landlady, who took most unkindly to what I had said and to such an extent that finally I was forced to seek other accommodation.

Many men at Crewe and other West Coast depots had a custom, of LNWR origin I believe, of pinning their 'slop jacket' (overall jacket) collar tight at the neck, so minimising the amount of coal-dust which could filter in. A neckerchief was often added to make doubly sure that nothing unwanted penetrated the inner regions.

Unlike the practice at ex-Midland sheds there was less evidence at Crewe of men wearing pre-grouping 'carry-overs' in the shape of badges and buttons. With the exception of one or two old LNWR war service badges and a few LNWR buttons on cap bands (not provided with the caps, so presumably attached by the loving wife) little remained. The LMS war service badges, however, were very common. Quite a number of older drivers in the top links carried their meals in the old-fashioned wicker baskets or in equally old 'tin-trunks', items commonly associated with enginemen of a bygone age. Pay day, however, continued the time-honoured ritual of first issuing the staff with brass checks (LNWR), which one exchanged for little tins containing one's money and pay slip.

Both North and South sheds at Crewe possessed handsome bronze plaques in memory of those who died in the 1914–1918 war, with their LNWR association well to the fore. These were greatly respected, kept polished and provided with vases of flowers from time to time and wreaths of poppies on November 11. The practice of attaching poppies to certain engines, customary at some West Coast sheds, did not appear to be practised at Crewe, however, though I believe the Crewe staff were responsible for smartening up either No 45500 *Patriot* or No 46170 *British Legion* and attaching wreaths to them, before despatching them to Rugby for the annual November 11 commemoration service.

I have purposely left the ex-Great Western Nantwich–Wolverhampton line until this point in my story, as while at Crewe I became particularly interested in this little one-time GWR outpost, set in the very heart of the former London & North Western empire. There was something quite mysterious about it until, by dint of a little research, I uncovered some reasons for the Great Western's arrival at Crewe. Between them two independent concerns had projected a railway from Wellington through Market Drayton to Nantwich. The GWR had seen in this line the possibility of tapping some valuable Mancheser traffic and so, by amalgamation in one case and a working agreement in the other (together with hard-won running powers over the LNWR from Nantwich to Crewe), the stranger was almost home. The line was opened throughout in November 1867, and became fully owned by the GWR in 1897.

Whether or not the Great Western really expected to build its own line onwards to Manchester, by way of Crewe, I cannot say, but they must have frightened the LNWR; indeed, local rumour at Crewe had it that Queens Park only came into existence in order to thwart any such GWR intention. However, the Great Western did obtain running powers to Manchester London Road for all trains, though these powers were to be used only if, in an independent arbitrator's opinion, the LNWR failed to provide proper facilities for Great Western Manchester traffic. Furthermore, it would appear that just before World War I the Great Western had come to satisfactory terms with the London & North Western, for an old GWR driver at Crewe for whom I fired remembered firing a GWR Bulldog 4–4–0, *Skylark*, on clearance tests from Crewe to both Manchester and Liverpool. What the outcome of this test was I do not know, but it may have resulted in the LNWR offering even better terms for GWR traffic.

That the GWR dug itself in quite firmly at Crewe is indisputable, for they had their own two-road engine-shed and special sidings. Engines, however, were turned either on the South Shed turntable or on the Gresty triangle. For many years the GWR had a separate locomotive allocation for Crewe, but from about 1930 the Crewe depot became merely a sub-shed for Wellington, which supplied all local engine requirements. The GWR paid a rental for the use of both the Gresty Lane sidings and also of Crewe station, from which the passenger trains were booked and handled by their own staff. Incoming GWR freight at one time ran straight into Basford Hall sidings, but latterly most of the trains terminated in Gresty down sidings. The GWR formerly marshalled their traffic with their own engines and staff, and Crewe GWR enginemen at one time had through workings to Worcester where they lodged, returning the following day, but for many later years they had not proceeded any further than to the Oxley sidings at Wolverhampton.

Despite being in the heart of London Midland territory, the (Great) Western enginemen at Crewe retained a remarkable Swindon outlook. In my LMR experience much of the practice I observed was alien, to say the least. There was something delightfully old-fashioned about their methods and practice. Long before I actually fired a WR locomotive, I was struck by the often comic appearance of their drivers—comic because of the way their overalls were usually worn. Presumably in compliance with (G)WR Rules and Regulations almost all WR men wore bicycle clips round the bottoms of their trousers. I never caught more than a glimpse of these clips, but suspect that somewhere they bore the GWR coat-of-arms and were probably produced in some part of Swindon works. The overalls were not, in fact, overalls at all, but consisted of separate trousers and jacket, unlike the normal bit-and-brace pattern common to other Regions. The trouser part was firmly secured by an unusually hefty pair of braces. Why these were so massive I am not sure, but I presume that they were provided for some dual purpose, perhaps to strap up ailing parts of an engine's anatomy, or maybe just to provide adequate support for the pockets, swollen as they often were by corks, split pins, rubber washers and sundry other possible requirements. To complete the picture, our hero probably grasped a large wad of cotton waste and, ten-to-one, displayed the GWR arms or initials somewhere on his person.

When working on the Western line conversation might often start with the question "Have you brought your handbrush?" Replying in the affirmative, I had now to face the engine, usually a Hall, Grange or 28XX p 2–8–0, the sight of which explained a lot about peculiar methods and practices. My experiences with these engines were infrequent enough for them to remain something of a novelty; they could both amuse and displease. The cabs had an impressive vastness about them, an illusion created by their height and spaciousness, while the latter effect was exaggerated by the absence of side-doors. The tenders were peculiar, for they retained the old-fashioned coal-well; none of that self-trimming nonsense here—brute force cost less! The cab fittings, apart from a few subtle differences, were arranged similarly to those of a Stanier engine. The illusion of simplicity created by the single water-gauge was destroyed by the presence of a brake of unusually fussy design, while the exhaust injector, dated in design, I should imagine, from Gifford's first patent! For added company the cab was provided with a sight-feed lubricator and, of course, the celebrated ATC gear. The equally celebrated vacuum pump (held, by the way, in the highest esteem) and the ATC bell and buzzer were new sounds for me to become used to; right-hand driving was, however, the same as in normal Derby practice and created no new problems.

Once on the road with a WR engine, I was soon shown how things were managed on this line. "None of your Midland slapdash here, my lad" was the rule. Flap up, flap down as each shovel (heavy and large by LMR standards) of coal was placed in the box on the haycock principle; neatly trim the coal and crack down to size for the next round; sweep the floorboards; take a brief spell on the hose—then start again. One had to conform, for the engines we relieved at Oxley were handed over in splendid order, with the cabs scrupulously clean, the fire in good shape and the coal all ready for the next firing. That these enginemen cared for their engines was obvious from the way that they carefully pointed out to relieving crews any little troubles the engine might have. The WR fireman, dressed in the same quaint way as the driver, always seemed to possess a large number of spare gauge glasses—enough, I used to think, to pipe a goodly part of any town's water supply. How many broken glasses WR engines had per trip I do not know, but on my runs they remained well-behaved, no doubt because I was a stranger. The Swindon breed of locomotives seemed inordinately thirsty creatures, for one rarely passed a water column without the tender being topped up; rather amusing, really, I thought, and rather like dogs and trees—but in reverse, so to speak.

Despite all this, I had some very happy times on the Oxley vacuums with WR engines, and my favourite engine was No 6803, a Grange 4–6–0 and a really splendid machine. As previously mentioned, the line between Nantwich and Wellington was moderately graded, the only incline of any note being the 1 in 104 up to Market Drayton Junction, approaching Wellington. Once on the main line there was a short pull up through Oakengates (so named, I believe, because of a thick oak gateway to the old walled Roman city) to Hollinswood sidings, from which the line fell at 1 in 150 for 5 miles past Shifnal to Cosford, then rising again at 1 in 137–100 for 4 miles almost to Codsall. Easy gradients completed the run to Oxley. Little steam was usually required after Hollinswood, momentum providing much of the energy required to tackle the final ascent from Cosford.

On being relieved at Oxley we retired to an old coach body which served as a relief cabin. We often had an hour or two to wait for the return working, usually from Didcot or Worcester, and I remember some splendid snoozes enjoyed here. Moreover, during a week's work I had over the line one springtime, I well remember awaking in the old coach to the most beautiful bird song I have ever heard. Set as it was in the middle of a hedgerow here and there scented with wild flowers, the coach was a wonderful place in which to relax.

Returning from Oxley there was some hard collar work to Hollinswood, but after this little further effort was called for. This line, with its customs and history, was certainly a favourite of mine. On one holiday occasion I worked on a light engine from Wellington to Shrewsbury, thereby linking up the third arm of the Crewe–Wellington–Salop triangle.

While at Crewe I noted a surprisingly large number of GW locomotive types—22XX 0–6–0s, 28XX 2–8–0s, 43XX 2–6–0s, 51XX 2–6–2 tanks, 57XX pannier tanks, and Castle, Hall. Grange and Manor 4–6–0s, and what I am almost certain was a County 4–6–0 coming off the Wellington line near Nantwich one day while I myself was working past on a Salop job. From time to time repairs were done to WR locomotives at both the North and South sheds and, by some curious arrangement, the 9.10am slow to Shrewsbury (incidentally the only passenger turn worked by the South Shed) was frequently powered by a WR 43XX, Hall or Castle. Even more odd was the fact that an ex-GW Crewe driver was usually provided as pilotman with these 'strangers'. To reduce the number of men so required Shrewsbury, which provided the engine for the job, tried to diagram standard types rather than WR engines, but from my own observation with but partial success.

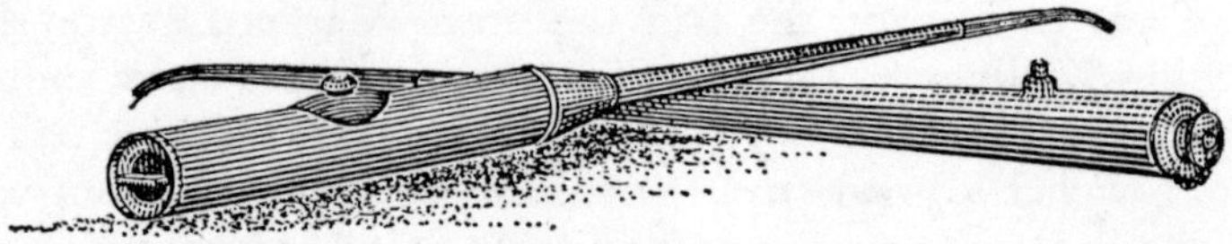

12

Lessons and Thoughts on Firing

How did you fire such and such a locomotive? How did you like this or that locomotive? These and countless similar questions I have tried to answer many times. Anyone who is at all interested in the subject can gain access to the rudiments of firing in any one of a number of text-books on the locomotive. In a few lines of cold print the whole art is reduced to a simplicity of basic rules, and to be fair, that is about all that can be done to aid the would-be fireman.

Practical experience has no substitute when it comes to firing a locomotive. It takes some time to tell at a glance the quality of coal provided and the varying methods of firing to use on different types of locomotive. Fundamentally there were three types of firegrate—the deep flat grate usually associated with tank shunting locomotives; the inclined grate of the older 0–6–0 and 4–4–0 types; and finally the two-part grate, horizontal near the firehole clear of the rear driving axle and thereafter inclined, which was in most common use on the later LMSR locomotives. It will be easy to appreciate that the first two grates were somewhat easier to fire than the two-level style last-mentioned.

In the first case, the flat grate required firing all over, or, alternatively, an artificial bank under the firehole door could be created to assist the coal to work down all over the grate. The latter was much the more usual on shunting engines, to avoid too frequent firing while to-and-fro shunting movements were taking place, and also to keep to a minimum the emission of smoke by too frequent charges of fresh fuel.

The inclined grate was fairly straightforward to fire. The slope provided tended to keep the fire on the move, gradually working towards the front of the grate and thereby making it necessary to fire most of the coal under the door and down the sides. The ideal combustion on this type of grate was obtained by the gradual movement of the fire and the natural burning away of fuel, thus considerably easing the fireman's work. Care had to be exercised to ensure that not too deep a fire built up under the brick arch up at the front of the grate.

The third type of grate was at first quite difficult to master, the junction of the two sections being hard to keep sufficiently covered with fire, particularly when a light fire was being carried, and when a violent slip in a few seconds could rip holes in such a fire. Whatever the grate employed, the combustion of coal was usually greater down the sides and under the door. This being so, it was obviously important to keep these points well supplied. Conversely, the draught in the centre of any grate was somewhat less, and this part could usually be relied on to be self-feeding from both sides and from the back of the box.

A less common variety of grate is that provided on the Pacifics. Though shorter than the usual narrow grates these were much wider, and firing them was rather a dual action, up and down and side to side. Thus it will readily be understood that firing a wide grate could become very arduous. The considerable width of such grates made for difficulty in keeping the back corners well supplied, and was often the major cause of steam shortage in such types. Some firemen filled the back corners of Pacific grates with lumps of brick arch to avoid keep filling them up.

Whatever type of grate was employed, the same general care in fire preparation was essential. Having checked the water-level in the boiler, the fire was spread evenly over the grate and was examined to see that it was free from dirt and clinker. It was always a good policy to 'feel' under the firebox door and back corners with the dart, to ensure that all clinker had been removed from these areas. Satisfied that the grate was evenly covered with clean fire and that the arch and tubes were clean and sound, the building up of the fire commenced. This was dictated to a certain extent by the type of coal provided. Good lump coal could be put on in quite large quantities, in the full knowledge that sufficient air space between the lumps would exist to aid rapid combustion. Small coal and coal of poor quality required much smaller amounts to begin with and might even require a few shovelsful of broken brick arch or limestone to gather the clinker and keep the bars free.

Whatever the coal, however, the rear of the grate would require most attention, by keeping the front bright and allowing the arch to get nice and hot, so that a few shovelsful just at the start of a run would bring the boiler up to full pressure. Most firemen would recognise the foregoing as elementary advice; unfortunately, however, it was not always possible to ensure that the above conditions could be adhered to. Frequently the shed steam-raisers would have filled the firebox with a large quantity of fresh coal, which would not allow the fireman to do more than spread his fire and open the dampers, while trusting that somehow the fire would be sufficiently burned through at the start of the run. In other cases the fire might have been lit for some 24 hours and would be anything but clean to start with.

The precise quantity of coal to have in the firebox prior to a run was dependent on the nature of the duty to be performed. In practice it was usually more than one would normally run with, to allow for settling of the firebed and to obtain the hottest fire possible without introducing much fresh coal at the start of a run. The only danger in having too much fire built up on shed came if, for any reason, the engine failed at the last minute. This happened on a number of occasions, and then a large fresh fire was not appreciated by the firedroppers!

The passed cleaner, when first put to firing, probably found his shovel rather heavier than he imagined, and took some time to adjust his stance to the rolling and pitching of the engine. The ideal was to keep the feet firmly apart, while relying on the shovel and its swing to shoot the coal into the firebox. The initial temptation was to move the feet too much, with the risk of missing the firehole or falling over. In time he would cure this, and learn gently to sway his body in such a way as to correct his balance each time the engine lurched. The usually circular firehole required the shovel to be directed accurately at each firing to avoid the edge of the blade catching the side of the firehole ring, with consequent spillage. Some firemen began to cure this by aiming not for the 'ring piece' but straight on to a specially-prepared coal 'shelf' built up just under the door. This not only made the aim surer, but on long boxes it shortened the distance the coal had to travel when projected off the shovel. Using this method, extra care was necessary to avoid the hands and forearms being burned by contact with the firehole itself and the baffle-plate.

Perhaps the young fireman's greatest problem, however, was learning to fire from both sides of the cab. In the larger cabs of the more modern locomotives this was not much of a problem, as there was quite enough room for him to fire from right or left of the cab, but on older engines—compound 4–4–0s and 4F 0–6–0 goods engines, for example, or LNW 0–8–0s —the fireman had only just enough room to work opposite the driver, be it right- or left-hand side. Most firemen, being right-handed, found firing from the right side of the cab awkward, the swing of the shovel taking a while to master, and the longer the grate the more awkward was the swing. A fireman soon got attached to a particular type of shovel, short or long, straight or angled, though the type of engine he had to work on to some extent imposed its own requirements. Most tank engines and the smaller, older tender engines gave only enough room to use a short shovel. At the other extreme, only a raw cleaner would normally attempt to fire the longest and widest grates with a short shovel. The use of gloves during firing was optional (provided the fireman supplied them). Gloves, however, made a shovel just that much more difficult to hold, the action of the glove tending to make the wooden shaft very smooth, and slipping sometimes resulted in the loss of this valuable item in the firebox—a sobering if not disastrous happening on a long run.

Text-books on handling locomotives usually advise firing on the road to be conducted on the principal of little and often—or controlled interval firing, depending on the type of engine, some four to eight shovelsful at a time, at up to two-minute intervals. In practice this was not often found acceptable, and a study on locomotive firing on the LMRegion elucidated some interesting facts. During the study the work of some 113 firemen was observed, and of these five only practised controlled firing. The classes of locomotives involved were: Class 2P Standard 4–4–0; Class 4P Compound 4–4–0; Class 5P and 6P 4–6–0; Class 8P 4–6–2 and 8F 2–8–0; and Garratt. The minimum and maximum shovelsful per firing, together with the time interval between firing, were as follows:

Table I

Engine	*Shovelsful Per Firing*			*Time Interval between Firings (min)*		
CLASS	AVERAGE	MINIMUM	MAXIMUM	AVERAGE	MINIMUM	MAXIMUM
2(std)	8.9	4.5	15.4	9.3	3.6	23.8
4(comp)	8.8	5.4	17.7	4.5	2.4	8.1
5	10.5	7.5	29.8	5.7	1.7	20.3
6P	9.3	4.6	16.3	3.8	2.1	7.0
8F	12.9	6.1	30.4	8.8	3.6	27.5
8P	18.8	10.5	43.5	7.0	4.7	18.9
Garratt	20.7	19.8	21.9	9.5	7.1	11.3

Table II showing variations in shovelling noted on 8 runs with the down Royal Scot worked by 8P locomotives. For kindly allowing the inclusion of these tables I am indebted to the Director of Operational Research, British Railways Board. They show the variation of firing rate practised by firemen and explain, to some extent at least, how an optimum rate of firing is hard to define.

Table II

Variation in Shovelling Rates

Eight Runs with Down Royal Scot (Class 8P Locomotive)

Portion of Run		*Run*							
		1	2	3	4	5	6	7	8
Euston to Tring	Shovels	112	121	141	133	117	126	113	199
	Minutes	38	40	42	39	39	39	37	40
	Shovs/Min	2.9	3.0	3.4	3.4	3.0	3.2	3.1	5.0
Tring to Bletchley	Shovels	54	16	30	34	36	33	83	30
	Minutes	14	13	14	15	15	14	15	15
	Shovs/Min	3.9	1.2	2.1	2.3	2.4	2.3	5.5	2.0
Bletchley to Rugby	Shovels	112	141	102	123	105	97	84	58
	Minutes	33	37	32	35	36	34	33	37
	Shovs/Min	3.4	3.8	3.2	3.5	2.9	2.9	2.5	1.6
Rugby to Tamworth	Shovels	107	125	71	118	76	102	93	80
	Minutes	27	28	26	26	29	26	25	28
	Shovs/Min	4.0	4.5	2.7	4.5	2.6	3.9	3.7	2.9
Tamworth to Whitmore	Shovels	148	128	131	144	136	96	178	146
	Minutes	48	37	37	39	39	38	38	37
	Shovs/Min	3.1	3.5	3.5	3.7	3.5	2.5	4.7	3.9
Whitmore to Weaver Jcn.	Shovels	71	50	64	68	84	77	65	57
	Minutes	28	26	41	27	30	33	32	28
	Shovs/Min	2.5	1.9	1.6	2.5	2.8	2.3	2.0	2.0
Weaver Jcn. to Wigan	Shovels	48	84	85	32	53	46	76	37
	Minutes	21	29	21	21	21	22	21	20
	Shovs/Min	2.3	2.9	3.9	1.5	2.5	2.1	3.6	1.9
Wigan to Lancaster	Shovels	136	166	152	176	102	131	132	140
	Minutes	44	41	49	49	40	40	47	42
	Shovs/Min	3.1	4.0	3.1	3.6	2.6	3.3	2.8	3.3
Lancaster to Oxenholme	Shovels	122	80	72	118	79	80	79	79
	Minutes	20	17	17	20	19	17	20	18
	Shovs/Min	6.1	4.7	4.2	5.9	4.2	4.7	4.0	4.4
Oxenholme to Tebay	Shovels	91	70	70	81	87	66	90	78
	Minutes	15	15	16	16	18	16	18	18
	Shovs/Min	6.1	4.7	4.4	5.1	4.8	4.1	5.0	4.3

Portion of Run		*Run* 1	2	3	4	5	6	7	8
Tebay to Shap Summit	Shovels	42	28	54	59	46	—	45	14
	Minutes	8	9	9	9	8	10	10	9
	Shovs/Min	5.3	3.1	6.0	6.6	5.8	—	4.5	1.5
Shap Summit to Carlisle	Shovels	41	22	26	30	16	12	71	22
	Minutes	30	31	31	30	31	30	30	34
	Shovs/Min	1.4	0.7	0.8	1.0	0.5	0.4	2.4	0.6
Total* for Run	Shovels	1043	1009	972	1086	921	854	1038	918
	Minutes	296	292	304	296	294	289	296	292
	Shovs/Min	3.5	3.5	3.2	3.7	3.1	3.0	3.5	3.1
Total for Run*	Mean Deviation from Firing Rates	1.05	0.87	0.87	1.15	0.80	0.71	0.92	1.10

* Euston to Shap Summit.

The fireman's general aim was to keep the grate evenly fed. He would soon discover how many shovelsful at a time were needed to cover any particular grate; 6, 8 or 12 would generally be enough to cover any size of grate. He had to bear in mind that heat was the prime factor, as the hotter his fire, the better the steaming. The whiter a coal fire burned, the better it was and he aimed to keep his fire in this condition, with no section of the grate over-fired and, therefore, choked. The colour of the fire and colour of the exhaust at the chimney were the main guides to the steaming of the boiler. Smoke (not dense) evenly leaving the chimney would indicate even coverage, but if the chimneys seemed to be smoking more to one side or the other, it would be an indication of a shortage of fuel or perhaps an excess somewhere. The smell of various exhausted smokes also could indicate whether the fire was clean or becoming choked with clinker, and an acid smell nearly always indicated the latter.

Correct use of the dampers when firing was all important. Small engines usually had only a front damper but larger engines two or more, at intervals below the grate. Many firemen used only the front damper and almost always left the others severely alone. I must say, however, that dampers were not fitted merely as ornaments and often partial opening of both gave a more even draught. To use dampers fully open was not usually necessary, one-third to one-half open being usually quite sufficient. Official method of firing locomotives were not, of course, the only ways of firing any particular type, and firemen soon developed their own individual methods, some preferring thicker and others thinner fires.

Water consumption had also to be considered. Once the train was under way, and with the fire really hot full pressure had almost been reached, it was time to set the injector boiler feed to approximately the rate of steam consumption; this, at any rate, was the theory. Practice, however, often decrees something different. To allow the maximum time for the fire to become hot the fireman, as a rule, would have as much water in the boiler at the start as the engine would safely permit. Allowing for steam space and the possibility of priming, the water would almost always be out of sight in the top of the glass. This allowed something like a mile or so before a further supply of water needed to be admitted. The injector was designed, not only to feed the boiler, but to adjust the rate of feed. Were injectors guaranteed to do the latter, all would be well, but in practice they rarely did so—they were on or off, delivering a fixed rate of water or none at all. With the injectors designed in most cases to feed the boiler at above the maximum steaming rate, this system of boiler feed tended to cool the boiler rather too much and to reduce the steam pressure. More simply, this means that at full pressure, say 225lb per sq in, the injector would be started and on reduction of pressure to about 210lb the injector would be stopped, having more than maintained the water level in the boiler required to recuperate the pressure.

After our fireman had mastered his fire and boiler feed, he still had plenty to keep him occupied. Large lumps of coal required breaking up to permit of better combustion, while the coal delivery shelf had to be kept free and not allowed to become jammed with lumps. Frequent damping of the cab floor was needed to stop the dust from rising, and there was watering the coal for the same purpose, interrupted occasionally, perhaps, by operating the water-scoop over troughs. A watch had to be kept on the lubricator (if any) in the cab, and eyes had to be used to assist the driver to read signals, and keeping the train under observation with periodical backward glances. Then a look-out had to be kept for a shifted load, an open door or a hot box. All these duties and firing at a rate of something like eight shovelsful every two minutes would keep the fireman more than fully occupied.

Some of the main LMSR locomotive classes now need individual consideration. The LMSR was perhaps fortunate in having, broadly speaking, a greater degree of standardisation than any line other than the Great Western. Possessed as was the former of large numbers of Class 4F 0–6–0s and Class 5 4–6–0s allocated throughout the region, most firemen were well acquainted with the methods required to work these types. The Class 5 was undoubtedly everyone's friend, a simple robust engine which required only average skill to produce sufficient steam. The 'Black Stanier' could be fired in numerous ways and responded well to all of them. It was not over-fussy as to what kind of coal it consumed, and even with a fair amount of clinkering was still capable of keeping going. Produced at intervals over something like 20 years, the class 5 4–6–0s by degrees had been improved. The earlier engines incorporated certain peculiarities of fittings evolved in the early period of the Stanier *régime*, which had seen later modifications.

Dampers were a case in point. The older version, arranged in a quadrant and slotting in a ratchet, were very inferior, not securing the damper flap properly and often jamming. The exhaust injectors fitted to the earlier engines also were inferior to those provided on the later ones, being much more prone to wastage and failure. Despite the fact that the frames and boilers of Class 5s were frequently switched, there was a distinct difference between the 50XX, 51XX, 52XX, 53XX, 54XX series and the 46XX and 47XX series. The 50XX and 52XX engines in particular became rough very quickly, as a rule, while the 46XX series continued smoothly for many months after shopping.

Whether anything was gained by fitting Caprotti valve-gear to Class 5s is open to question. I firmly believe that they were not as good in this form, nor can I say that roller bearings made them noticeably better runners than ordinary Class 5s. Certainly no engine throughout the length and breadth of the LMSR commanded the same respect as did the 'Black Stanier'. Enginemen swore by them. My own experiences on Western Region Hall and Grange 4–6–0s and, to a very limited extent, on Eastern Region B5 4–6–0s more than satisfied me that the '5' was the better engine, especially for steaming and cab comfort.

The numerous Class 4F 0–6–0 goods was a much more controversial locomotive. This no doubt was due to its Derby characteristics, which were not appreciated very much by the older generation of LNWR and LYR division men. My experience indicated that, on the whole, the older MR engines and Derby-built locomotives were better steamers and freer runners than those from Horwich or Crewe works, the 45XX series being the most temperamental for steam. The best examples in the class were the few with tall chimneys (indicated by a blue circle on the cab sides) and they usually steamed very well indeed. The older MR engines were almost all shopped at Derby, and some drivers insisted that Derby set the valves differently from Crewe and Horwich. This may indeed be so, because I cannot believe that Derby supplied each 4F with a guardian angel or used any other magical persuasion!

Some of the MR engines and others boasted a Derby-type exhaust injector of the same type as that fitted to the compounds, the Fowler 2–6–4 tanks and, I believe, the 'Crab' 2–6–0s. These injectors were not very strong and gave frequent trouble, the usual footplate practice being to rely on the live-steam injector only. Some of the MR engines had the old chain-and-flap type of firehole door, a very awkward piece of equipment which was not easy to open and close in a hurry. With this type, the main door fell horizontally away from the hole, sometimes at the most inconvenient moments. It worked in conjunction with a flap at the top edge to regulate the admission of air. This ungainly piece of equipment was not very helpful when the engine was at all shy for steam, being either open or shut and not making for quick firing, as over a half-flap. The hinge frequently became jammed with small coal, requiring the flap to be flicked up and down to remove the obstructions.

All 4Fs had two features in common, a gap between the floor and the firebox back-plate which caused clouds of dust to swirl up when the engine was moving, despite wedges of sacks and old clothing stuffed in to block this space, and a roof gutter which deflected the rain in a stream down one's neck or back. However, comfort was of secondary importance on the 4F, for the art of keeping going was generally a full-time occupation. Personally I learned to treat the 4F with the greatest of respect. If circumstances allowed, I built the fire up very carefully, mainly under the door, and kept firing at frequent intervals, about four shovelsful at a time. Firing too heavily only caused the firebox to choke with smoke and a heavy black fug to roll out of the chimney while steam pressure fell rapidly. The grate was so inclined that coal needed do no more than just get inside the door, with a little placed down each side. At best, the fire could be so thin at the front as to be literally hopping about on the grate, but this was hard to achieve, and with poor coal the front of the grate soon became clogged with dirt and steaming became much impaired.

The parallel boilers of these engines seemed more susceptible to dirt and priming than did taper boilers—this goes for all MR-type parallel boilers—and the method of boiler feed delivery was more cooling than top feed. The ancillary fittings—blower, steam heat supply and injectors—were a great drain on the boiler and working a passenger train with a 4F 0–6–0 was quite an experience. They rode quite well, however, and MR men usually adored them, defending them at every stage. Other men put up with them or despised them, and LNW men much preferred their 0–8–0s. All in all, the 4F was a most controversial engine, which personally I found to be too temperamental and unreliable.

The three-cylinder Jubilee and Patriot Class 4–6–0s were fundamentally the same design of locomotive, but with different types of boiler. The

Jubilee, or 5X type, as it was more generally known, was regarded as little more than a Class 5 with larger driving wheels, but this, perhaps, oversimplified the issue. True, they were a better engine than a 5 at high speed —over 80mph—but with that one advantage they were not regarded as much superior. Midland division enginemen regarded them highly, but I cannot say the same for those of the Western division. Apart from the engines used on the two-hour Euston–Birmingham expresses, the 5Xs on the Western division were relatively scarce and very much under the shadow of the more powerful Royal Scots.

Why the 5X was so popular on the Midland Division is a matter for conjecture. For years there were no more than three Royal Scots on the Midland Division at Holbeck for the Leeds–Glasgow run, so there was little chance for any comparisons. For myself I found the Jubilees temperamental, with a very finicky appetite. Few would burn much coal under the arch and they usually ceased to steam as soon as sparks ceased to leave the chimney; the emission of sparks meant that the fire was thin under the arch. They were heavy on water and could become very rough riders. Many 5Xs had old Fowler 3500gal tenders; these in themselves were poor riders and caused, I was told, quite a lot of injector trouble by small coal working under the fall-plate—an ailment not so common on the engines with the larger tenders. As to their water consumption, I frequently found it necessary to use both injectors at once—a practice I only favoured on the very best of steamers!

As to their steaming capacity, an interesting test was conducted on a 5X on the Rugby test plant in the early 1950s. Briefly, the example under test with a given grade of coal produced less steam than standard Class 5 and ER Class B1 4–6–0s. A double-chimney standard Class 4 4–6–0 even bettered the Jubilee output. Modifications involving trials with both improved single-chimney and double-chimney engines corrected this steaming trouble, but few of the engines were subsequently modified in the same way. Similar results, with improved draughting, were obtained on a 4F 0–6–0, though again, however, never adopted as standard practice. I always firmly believed that only half the grate of a 5X was really burning coal, the other half merely storing hot cinders. But I did not like the Jubilees much and usually regarded them as inferior to my beloved Baby Scots or Patriots. If I could have had my own engine regularly, I would certainly have booked one of the latter for a while.

The boiler of a Patriot could be every bit as awkward as that of a Jubilee, but in many cases this was due to priming, or what seemed to be the parallel boiler weakness—excessive scaling. True, a Patriot smokebox sometimes leaked air, and Patriots seemed to have an asthmatical front end, but when thoroughly warmed up the old Baby Scot was a grand engine. General opinion was not so favourable, however; many firemen found these engines poor steamers, while drivers of the Crewe–Carlisle fitted freights were not exactly envied when accompanying these charges. Given a clean boiler and a tight smokebox I still preferred the parallel boiler to the Stanier Taper type, and could say the same of the 2–6–0 'Crabs'. For all the wonders of taper boilers, they never seemed to have the same reserve, nor could they be rallied as quickly as a parallel boiler. This personal view, however, is one which would not have been shared by every LMR engineman.

One of the finest 4–6–0 designs ever evolved must be the rebuilt Royal Scot. These splendid engines never ceased to amaze me and next to the Duchess Pacifics they were the most competent express passenger engines on the LMR. Their boiler power was enormous, providing one could keep up with what was certainly a good appetite; the double blast pipe tended to make the fire burn more evenly all over the grate, resulting in a healthy demand at the front of the box and under the arch. For heavy work they would require a very thick fire, particularly at the back of the grate. Care was needed to ensure that heavy fires were run down somewhat when working lightly (down the bank from Tring, for instance) as when well notched up they had not sufficient blast to keep a thick fire really hot. One of their most important features was their economy in water consumption —particularly at three-quarters-of-a-glass and under. This was a great advantage whenever the boiler needed to rally steam and got me out of difficulty several times—a difficulty, I may add, created by my own inability to stand too much continuous labour 'up-front' of the grate.

They never seemed to me to be particularly rough riders (compared at any rate with the Compounds), possibly because they kept a fireman rather too busy to think much about comfort. Although a straightforward design of engine, they needed care in both driving and firing and fixed cut-offs were taboo if good performances were needed. There was little general complaint about the Scots, except perhaps from some enginemen who were natural grumblers anyway. Most LMSR drivers I knew preferred a rebuilt Royal Scot to a Britannia 4–6–2, though they would welcome the latter's superior fuel capacity, especially on the Holyhead–London run.

Some enthusiasts have suggested to me that a rebuilt Patriot 4–6–0 was superior to a Royal Scot, but I have yet to hear anything to substantiate this claim. To enginemen all the 7Ps were the same—with the exception, perhaps, of No 46170, the first of the rebuilds, which did seem to be above average in hauling capacity, even if below par in the matter of smooth riding. Off the footplate it is possible that the Royal Scots were not quite the grand engines that they appeared to be in service. Repairs, I believe, were generally heavier than they perhaps ought to have been, but one must remember that they were rebuilds and not a completely new design. My own feeling was that they were slightly top-heavy and as a result, not in the 100mph class. Schedules, however, rarely demanded anything like such a speed as this, though a maximum of 100mph was recorded, with one of them on the Midland Division. Boilerwise, I think they were the most successful narrow-box design ever constructed in this country, with plenty of reserve. I had no experience of the old parallel-boiler Royal Scots, but I heard little complaint of these except perhaps that they tended to get rough quickly. Unlike the rebuilt Royal Scot the older boiler burned most coal just under the door.

An interesting point about the rebuilds concerned the amount of their original inside motion that was retained. This varied to some degree from engine to engine, some having a much heavier type of inside crosshead than others. Most, if not all, Royal Scots were fitted with rocking grates and self-cleaning smokeboxes. To me one of their happier features was the original design of cab side-sheet, with cut-away windows. With due deference to Great Western enthusiasts, I could *never* imagine Castles or Kings storming out of Euston on the duties that the Royal Scots regularly handled, and working to the common-user and big diagram workings that the Royal Scots were wont to do.

Next we come to the ultimate in LMR passenger power, the Duchess and Princess Royal 4–6–2s. I well remember my first run on a Duchess, not just because it was to me an event, but because I was immediately aware of greater power than I had ever believed a steam engine could possess. I looked upon these monsters then as Rolls-Royces among engines, supremely strong and effortless in action. They would simply purr along and rarely, to my own admittedly limited experience, were they opened out to any extent. Often I felt that anything was possible with a Duchess fully extended and over the right kind of road, free of checks. But such idyllic conditions were not to be found on the LMR and restraint generally had to be a feature of their every-day operation. To have obtained the full benefit of the design I consider that these engines might well have been candidates for mechanical stokers. Feeding 50 sq ft of grate for any distance is no child's play and skill was not the only operative requirement; sheer grit and guts were needed to stoke them regularly, day in and day out. Frequently I met men who, one time or another, had been firemen at Camden (there was such a one at Lancaster), but had resigned from the footplate or removed to a more leisurely depot, accusing the demands of the 4–6–2s as being partly responsible. Brilliant though the Duchesses were in action, I never ceased to feel that they were a little too much for manual firing.

Of the earlier Princess Royal Pacifics I had no experience, but they were certainly not held in the same esteem as the Duchesses; indeed, the general opinion at Crewe was one of dislike. To judge from the repairs carried out at North Shed they dropped their inside motion too frequently, and they could also be poor steamers requiring very careful firing and driving to produce their best. Age was beginning to tell, and drastic rebuilding or perhaps replacement was overdue. All in all, a Princess Royal lacked the best features of a Duchess—lighter valve-gear, superior front-end design, a good-steaming boiler coupled with double blast, rocking-grate and coal-pusher although one or two Princesses did have lighter valve-gear. Apart from their behaviour on the road, preparing them, and particularly oiling up, were thoroughly disliked, No 46200 and, I believe, No 46201, being particularly troublesome, as they had more oiling points than any other LMR engine, in complete contrast to No 71000 which had hardly any. The reputation of the Princess Royals can be better understood by the fact that the Crewe enginemen bitterly complained if one of them was rostered instead of a Duchess for one of the more exacting 8P duties. This applied in particular to the Perth duties, on which two Class 5 4–6–0s were much preferred if no Duchess was available.

Enginemen, by and large, are a conservative crowd, not given to discussing their job and locomotives in particular, unless they really have a grievance. Crewe North mess-room witnessed many a fierce discourse on the exacting Princess Royals; but even these were infinitely preferable to the experimental poppet-valve Pacific, No 71000. This engine was the black sheep of the LMR Pacific stud, with a fearful reputation for coal and water consumption. Between bouts of activity it spent long periods inactive, either under repair or awaiting spares. Even in the best conditions it proved to have no advantage over a Duchess. (It was banned on the Perth runs eventually.)

Of the 2–6–4 tanks I had little personal experience, and with a great dislike of enclosed cabs I never regarded them too favourably. Nevertheless they were very competent machines, rode well and generally steamed well. The injectors on the Stanier, and more so on the Fairbairn tanks, were tricky pieces of equipment, prone to blowing back at the slightest brake application. Furthermore, they were not easy to adjust to maximum feed, any other setting proving quite insufficient. Taking water at speed in forward running position required no small amount of skill to avoid being drowned in the overflow, which sometimes broke open the front windows. Perhaps their worst feature was the rectangular 'coal tunnel' fed from the bunker, which, with large lump coal, had a nasty habit of jamming at a critical moment. All in all, however, the 'big tanks' were accepted as quite satisfactory engines.

Of 2–6–0s we had four basic types. By far the most popular were the

Fowler 27XX Class, or 'Crabs'. Of squat, ungainly appearance, they were excellent mixed traffic locomotives, provided the mixture did not require too much passenger work. Their gently-sloping grates were easy to fire, and they steamed quite well with poor coal or inexperienced firing methods. They were sure-footed, and rail conditions had to be very bad to make them slip much (the incident, recounted earlier, of a 'Crab' slipping badly on Lancaster Bank took place in the autumn when leaves from the tree-lined cutting lay over the rails). While not too happy at much over 60mph (when they could 'wag' alarmingly) they were very strong—stronger than the Class 5s in fact, and, I was given to understand, very easy to maintain. Their injectors were weak, however, and could have done with replacement by a more powerful type. The cabs were large and quite comfortable, with funny little round stools 'growing' out of the cab floor.

Some of the earlier examples had excellent screw-adjusted dampers, were a great advance on the ordinary lever-and-ratchet arrangement, which usually tended to close when one was not looking. The standard type of flap on these locomotives almost filled the firehole. Three air-slits provided top air and tended also to draw the fire under the door, causing it to burn more freely than the standard LMR flap; this latter, owing to its smallness, tended to permit rather too much air over the 'hump' of the fire at the back, somewhat cooling it in consequence. The flap on the 'Crab' 2–6–0s did not however permit of coal being fed over the top as readily as the LMR standard type flap.

The Stanier version of the 'Crab' was not so widely distributed, and I never had much to do with them until I went to Crewe. Here they worked turn-and-turn-about with Class 8F's on freight, particularly to the Wirral and North Wales. I was perhaps unfortunate in my choice of engines, for they always seemed to be overdue for shops—loose, leaking and rough; furthermore, they seemed too rigid to my way of thinking, especially at speed. I had a marked preference for the parallel boiler of the 'Crabs' over the tapered ones on the Stanier engines; the two-angled grate of the latter was harder to work with. They were not in themselves poor steamers—they merely required a little more care. Many of these engines had the awful 'quadrant' dampers, a relic from the earlier Stanier era, and one that could well have been done without. The remaining classes of 2–6–0 were the two post-war classes of Ivatt design. Personally I was not impressed with either, and least of all with the 4MT type. True, my experience with the latter was confined mainly to examples with the double chimney. They were not very good steamers and in double chimney form they were distinctly sluggish and heavy on water. Also they were dirty engines and for some reason or other had uncomfortably hot cabs.

Reference now is necessary to the 2–8–0s and 0–8–0s. Little needs to be said about the standard 2–8–0s, save that they were thoroughgoing freight engines of the best kind. I never had to fire a bad steamer, nor can I think of anything detrimental about them. During my footplate career I was able to compare them with the Austerity 2–8–0s and the GWR 28XX 2–8–0s. Of the Austerities, I have said enough about them elsewhere in this book. Although based on the GWR 28XX design, the Stanier 2–8–0 to my mind had the edge on the former in its economy both of fuel and water consumption as well as being of a more modern design.

Of the two main 0–8–0 classes, the Fowler 495XX (or 'Austin 7'), I rarely came by, certainly not often enough to form any clear-cut opinion, save that for the crew they possessed many of the usual MR characteristics. Not so, however, the ex-LNW 0–8–0s; a few lessons firing these gained from me the warmest sympathy for all one-time LNW men. The LNW cab fittings were an abomination. I always thanked my lucky stars that I did not start on the footplate at Bescot or Spring Branch; had I done so I should probably have resigned very quickly and this book would doubtless not have been written.

Crewe drawing office seemed to have had one thing uppermost in mind when designing the cab details on these engines, and it was to make things as difficult and inaccessible as possible. The brake and injectors were both tucked out of the way and the tender coal-shelf was neatly guarded by two wheels—one for the brake and the other for the water-scoop, both placed in such a position as to make firing extremely difficult. The sloping cab floor, with a small channel to the firehole and flanked by two deep platforms, was composed of wood block flooring, conveniently lodging all the spilt coals and extremely difficult to clean. As shelter the cab was little short of futile, being only half the apparent depth, thanks to the extension of the firebox back-plate into the cab. The fall-plate between engine and tender formed a very necessary part of the firing platform, but as this was continuously rising and falling, the fireman had to be very smart on his feet to avoid being launched on to the track—there being, of course, no doors between engine and tender.

Most Midland-trained enginemen had trouble in making the LNW 7Fs steam, and I was no exception, having on at least one occasion less than 100lb of steam instead of the registered 175lb maximum working pressure. But unlike most locomotives, they did not take at all unkindly to this state of affairs, and would keep steadily plodding on. The LNW injector was a most ingenious product, with the steam valves located at the hottest point in the cab, and too hot to operate without gripping them with a cloth. They had no visible overflow, and regulating them was undertaken more by feel than anything else. Unlike most injectors, which provide a nice healthy sound when working properly, the LNW version had a barely audible muffled squeal. All this coupled with an antiquated brake system and a regulator working in reverse to normal practice (shut when normally open, and vice versa) made them a Heath Robinson dream of the first order.

Finally, a few remarks as to the BR Standard types. For myself I find it difficult to accept change for change's sake; when confronted, therefore, with the standard equivalent of the home product, scarcely advanced in efficiency in any respect yet incorporating many new and often less pleasant features, I formed a great dislike of Standards as a whole; though again restricted in my judgment by infrequent contact. To me they were as foreign as an Eastern Region B1 or a Western Hall. Suffice it to say that I never fired a Standard which could show any marked superiority over the LMS equivalent, and I have very conservative views when it comes to cab details—for me it was MR or LMR or nothing. It is a curious fact that the driver's controls are usually little noticed by his fireman, until the driver finds himself unable, alone, to manipulate them. This state of affairs was almost unknown to me until I worked on Standard designs, when I assumed a new duty, that of Chief Assistant Regulator manipulator and reverse 'screwer'. So far as the LM Region was concerned, but with one or two local exceptions, the Standards were not a significant factor anyway; they merely added variety to the engineman's daily round, though little in the way of excitement. These 'Heinz'-designed engines (as they were sometimes called) probably gave more pleasure to the design staff than to the footplate men, and I certainly had little enthusiasm for them.

So much for the main LMR locomotive classes; they were a hardy lot, basically sound, and, from the enginemen's point of view, robust and efficient. To me they were the best stud of steam engines in the country and collectively were head-and-shoulders above those of their competitors.

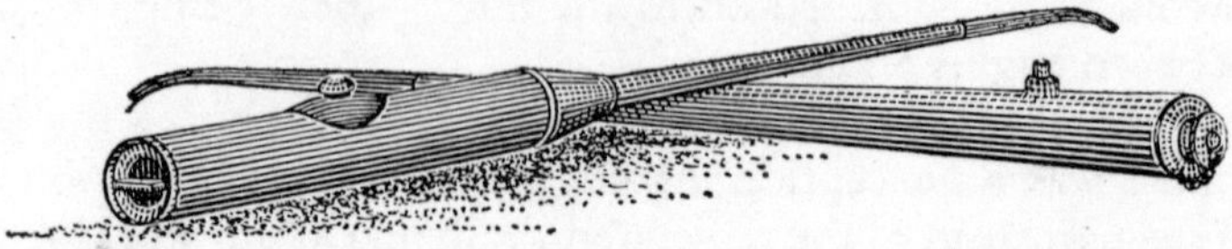

13

Compensations

Despite the rigours of locomotive firing, the footplate offered many hidden compensations. One rarely knew from day to day on what engine one would be booked next, and great was the feeling of pleasure to find, perhaps, that this was a recently overhauled and repainted machine standing proudly in its shining new coat of paint and providing that lovely smell of warm varnish, almost sufficient in itself to be taken as a good omen. More than this, such a sight instantly inspired one with the desire to spare no effort by tip-top firing to produce some first-class work.

It is difficult fully to convey the feeling of pride when backing slowly into a station and on to a train with a really smart engine. Passengers whose one thought was to reach their destination, porters who had seen it all before, even the most nonchalant of souls would stare in obvious admiration, some males showing by their nervous smiles and gleaming eyes their desire to fulfil their childhood ambition to ride on the engine. Respect, too, would seem to be indicated by the pleasantness of the guard, the politeness of the businessmen enquiring as to the booked arrival time, the deference of the restaurant car attendants when begging the driver to be careful when braking during the serving of the soup, or the sleeping car attendant's request that we should provide plenty of steam-heat.

This feeling of pride was heightened in the knowledge of the independence of the footplate. True, we had foremen and shedmasters, locomotive inspectors and stationmasters as overseers, but they were in evidence for very short periods of the working day only. This independence provided the basis for teamwork of the highest order, each member of the crew learning to anticipate almost exactly the next move and requirement of the other. This freedom of the footplate was very rewarding—for it meant that one could do one's own work with little or no interference and in the manner which one preferred. This solace of footplate life was a balancing factor to the barrage of noise and clatter that went on incessantly. In these conditions it might be difficult to imagine that peace could reign on the footplate, but this was in fact so.

Many a delightful hour have I wiled away, between spells of firing, lost in my thoughts, with my feet resting casually on the firebox back-plate, toasting my toes amid the flickering shadows created by the flames licking around the firehole and providing an alternating pattern of glowing shapes within the cab. These occasions were more frequently met with during lengthy sojourns in loops and sidings awaiting the approaching express. The return to reality came with the thunder of the express engine growing louder and louder, the very rails vibrating until, with an earth-shaking roar, the train sped past and was lost in the darkness.

Throughout the steam locomotive era innumerable people have been captivated by the tremendous sense of might and power conveyed by the sight and sound of locomotive, and particularly at speed. I was no stranger to this lore, and was impressed beyond words by the exhilaration of travelling at speed on a locomotive. This produced a state of near-delirium as with quickening pace I heard and felt the ring of the side-rods, the swaying of the cab, the pitching and rolling of the engine, the beat on the rails and, last but not least, the delightful purring of the exhaust—the whole creating a stirring blend of superlative power. At such times I would become a demon with my shovel crashing and ringing from tender to firehole, with coal transferred at a phenomenal rate from one to the other and with an urgent craving welling up inside me demanding more and more work. Make no mistake, this was no silly infatuation, but rather a gripping, almost supernatural tension, difficult to define or to reason, but something I frequently encountered. Needless to say this output of effort was so great that it completely removed any pent-up pressure previously apparent, and all such runs ended in a feeling of glorious relaxation.

To a certain degree all this could be attributed to the sense of purpose and satisfaction gained by the knowledge that through one's own efforts there was being provided the power by which the driver controlled everything the locomotive was doing, and this being so I certainly never felt inferior in any way to a driver. Indeed, I could feel his equal in importance.

The 'music' of the engine was but one of many delights. There was the sight of one's train snaking along behind, sweeping gently into curves, all so precise and orderly amid a wake of dust and smoke. This was punctuated from time to time by the biting tang of scorching brake-blocks—not in itself objectionable but rather the reverse, and emphasising still further a sense of speed and control over immense power that is not easily conveyed by any other type of machinery or mode of transport.

Naturally enough, the greatest pleasures of all were those enjoyed during actual running. The variety of country met with during my firing life was considerable, and the contrast on some runs often delightful.

Dawn or evening are by far the best times to discover real beauty in one's surroundings, and my work often provided this opportunity.

At dawn the countryside, particularly that of the fell country, was beyond question the finest of all. Early mornings on Shap and cloudless skies with the soft greys and greens, the patches of contrasting colour from heather-clad hillsides, whitewashed farmhouses, autumn-tinted woodland and hedgerow, the gentle golden colours of the dry broken ridges; for mile after mile the blues, greens and greys, the white foaming streams dashing down hillsides, the bridges clad in lichens, mosses and ivy, the embankments and cuttings massed with wild flowers, cowslips, violets, primroses and scented herbage; the tall pines, steep crags and mountain screes; the hillsides criss-crossed with walls of stone—all these at various times have been the delight of my footplate life. The same country, lashed with rain or blinding snow becomes wildly beautiful, unfriendly perhaps, but magnificent. Further south, towards Morecambe Bay, could be seen some of the most beautiful sunsets, with a brilliant deep orange sun fading into the sands and a purple-green streaked sky marking perhaps the end of another lovely summer's day.

With steam on and hard at work, the locomotive is perhaps an easy source of delight. The same can be said, also, when one is rolling downgrade with little more than a breath of steam, and with the brake the only instrument of correction and control. With ever-increasing speed, the effortless coasting of a locomotive round curves, rolling sweetly and effortlessly, was a superb contrast to the hours of effort previously with steam on and a staccato exhaust.

Speed alone was not the only purveyor of delight. There was the goods engine plodding slowly up-grade, with a column of exhaust shooting high into the sky, its deep brown colour sometimes set against a cloudless backcloth, and the blast deepening and echoing in the depths of cuttings and beneath overbridges to near-deafening proportions; these provided the confident assurance so typical of the freight locomotive.

Many more delights were seen from within my little citadel on the engine. There was the hurly-burly at the station, alive with people engaged in preparation for receiving trains, loading vans, trundling platform trolleys, sorting mail-bags, dispensing tea; with passengers waiting anxiously for their trains, amorous good-byes and sad-looking people setting out on reluctant journeys; not to mention scavenging pigeons and stalking station cats searching for their food.

At night-time the railway image to me was almost fairy-like, with its myriad lights—green, yellow, red and white signal lights; station and yard lights, engine lights, the confusing lights of highways; the friendly little lights in cottages tucked away amid the hills and valleys; the deep glow of towns and cities amid a sea of darkness—and the sensation of swaying, rolling and lurching, crashing over crossovers, hurtling through cuttings, under bridges and through tunnels, screaming through remote stations, with a roaring exhaust is one that will remain with me for the rest of my life, and one that I am thankful to have been fortunate to experience.

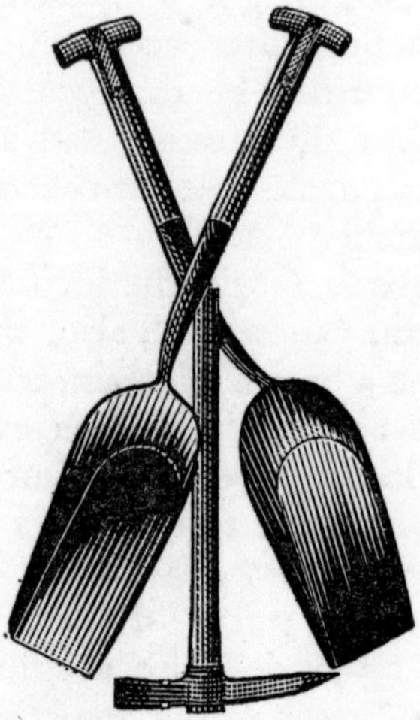

Index